PRACTICAL HANDGUN

TRAINING

A guide for the interested citizen on the practical and
functional aspects of handgun shooting and related
topics

by Richard P. Rosenthal
Chief of Police, Wellfleet MA, retired
Lieutenant, NYPD, retired

Other books by the author:

The Murder of Old Comrades

Sky Cops

K-9 Cops

Rookie Cop, Deep Undercover in the JDL
(Jewish Defense League)

Self-Publishing Simplified

Nogales, Sasabe, Lochiel, parts of the Third Nation

The Use of Force in Modern Policing

Table of Contents

Introduction

This work is aimed at both new students as well as firearms instructors. The goal of the book is to offer insight into various aspects of the basic mastery of the handgun, as well as practical instruction in several ancillary areas in regard the practical use of the sidearm. The material the book contains comes from my over forty years in the police field, including assignments within the NYPD's Firearms & Tactics Section, where I was responsible for conducting the Police Firearms Instructors School, the Heavy Weapons Training program and Research and Testing. I also had twelve years of field experience as an NYPD detective, serving, among my various assignments, in narcotics enforcement as well as in both homicide and robbery squads.

For the last thirty-five years of my police career, to varying degrees, I have been involved in firearms instruction. I'd like to share some of the knowledge I've gained through training, education and, most importantly, that which I've experienced through personal observation.

My education in this field came mostly from my time with the New York City Police Department's Police Academy Firearms and Tactics Section (FTS). During this period in the department's history there were over thirty thousand officers serving the city and the FTS expended approximately six million rounds a year in training and service use. I served in the unit as a sergeant and later in the rank of lieutenant, under three commanders:

Lt. Frank McGee. Frank made the unit what it is, a world class firearms training venue. He was a curmudgeon, a brilliant politician, somewhat of an authoritarian administrator with a soft spot in his heart for a subordinate's sob-story. I learned a great deal from Frank about the practical training of large numbers of mostly disinterested people in how to use firearms (instructing the students both <u>how</u> and <u>when</u> – thus the unit's name of *Firearms and Tactics Section*). Frank would say that just teaching a person how to use a firearm, without also teaching them proper tactics, is to give them only half a loaf. Frank was a good man to learn from.

Lt. Tom McTernan, a protégé of Frank's, and a man who also appreciated the very practical problems inherent in the training of large numbers of occasional firearms users. Tom co-authored the first of the popular <u>Street Survival</u> books. During my police career I always kept one of Tom's favorite admonitions in mind. Speaking about those officers who rose to the rank of administrator, making decisions that affected the lives of officers in the field, Tom would say, "We (the administrators) sit behind bullet-proof desks." His meaning was clear. The administrator making the decision wouldn't be the one facing the consequences of his directive. Be careful what dictates you come down with or you are likely to get people hurt.

Captain John Cerar. John was a good guy. He had no prior experience in the field of firearms training, thus his primary function at the unit was that of an administrator and as a "herder of cats," that is, the managerial oversight of the over one hundred members –all free spirits– of the Firearms and Tactics Section.

I hope that this book will serve two purposes; offering practical information on the subject of using the handgun for the newer shooter, while addressing issues that an experienced firearms instructor might find useful. This work is my attempt at distilling what information is necessary for a person to master who wishes to gain *Practical* and *Task Related* knowledge on the use of the handgun and its related gear, along with material designed for use by instructors, explaining in more detail the whys and justifications for the training as outlined by me. And while I speak of my observations while in police service at the FTS, in point of fact this book has been aimed more for the citizen firearms user.

With Captain John Cerar and the Master Firearms Instructors of the unit, December 31, 1986

Those last two concepts which I just mentioned, that of determining what training or equipment is both *Practical* as well as *Task Related*, is most important and requires additional discussion.

Both Frank and Tom taught me that there was an inclination on the part of firearms instructors to make training increasingly more difficult for their students. The problem is that in so doing the instructors frequently lost sight as to why the training was being given in the first place. The mantra of the Firearms and Tactics Unit while I was there was, stated simply, that whatever piece of equipment (firearm, holster, speedloader, etc.) was recommended, whatever tactic employed, had to meet the criteria of being both *Practical and Job Related.* And these recommendations had to be buttressed by actual data, preferably obtained from the officers in the field.

To put it another way, if the firearm was not practical for the occasional firearm's user to employ (the "occasional firearms user" being a description that fully fit more than 90% of line officers in the department), why was it being recommended? If the firearm model was not directly related to the task (job) at hand, the same question held true. Furthermore, as Tom would say, we at the FTS were safely sitting behind "bullet proof desks." Therefore, we had to make sure our decisions reflected the needs of the officers in the field, not the brainstorm of some highly interested hobbyist or some smug self-righteous bureaucrat.

As a professional firearms instructor I was often amused when intensely interested hobbyists would voice their views and opinions in regard what firearm should be carried by members of the NYPD. Time and again their words of wisdom would go something like; "When are you guys going to let us go over to the _____?" The blank to be filled in was frequently the firearm/caliber flavor of the day as seen in the popular hobbyist firearms magazines available on newsstands. Over the years I've heard heartfelt recommendations for the adoption of no less than these assorted calibers; 9x19mm (9mm Luger), .357 Magnum, .41 magnum, .44 Special, and the .45 ACP. The list of handguns the department was advised to adopt ranged from the Charter Arms Bulldog in .44 Special to the Colt 1911A1 semiautomatic pistol in .45 ACP (carried "cocked and locked" of course!).

So, how does one (whether an individual instructor or the head of a major firearms training facility, it matters not) determine which piece of equipment is suitable for his students to use? Simply put, this is done by examining the most relevant data available in regard that particular piece of equipment. We were quite fortunate in the NYPD in having significant informational resources at our disposal. That department is an enormous bureaucracy. Most all that happens in and around it is documented, filed and stored. Currently, there is the department's Firearms Discharge Report (colloquially referred to by its early title,

SOP-9 or Special Operating Procedure 9). This report was initiated by Frank MaGee and contains much minutiae regarding combat confrontations which take place between city officers and their adversaries. Indeed, reading the latest versions of the report, I find that its current writers seemed to have forgotten the reason it was first introduced and have come to believe that more is always better. Digging out truly useful, practical-to-apply information from the current iterations of the report proved to be a daunting task. None the less, the report remains worth reading.

A word of caution; the newest iteration of the report seems to have been designed to hide meaningful information rather than make it available to the report's readers. Instead of "hit potential," or, the number of rounds fired in relation to the number of hits made on target, there is a new assessment in its place, the *Objective Completion Rate*. From the report, here is the definition of this new measure:

Objective Completion Rate

The department does not calculate hit percentage when describing ID- AC* incidents, in part because it is sometimes unknown (for example, in cases when a subject flees) and also because of the widely differing circumstances in individual incidents. Instead, the NYPD uses what it calls "the objective completion rate per incident" because it is considered both more accurate and more informative. When an officer properly and lawfully perceives a threat severe enough to require the use of a firearm and fires at a specific threat, the most relevant measure of success is whether the officer ultimately stops the threat. This is the objective completion rate, and it is determined irrespective of the number of shots Firearms Discharges.

*(Note: ID-AC = Intentional Discharge-Adversarial Conflicts)

*

The evaluation of officer involved shootings now appears to permit a situation, such as a hypothetical shooting in which an officer discharges his/her sidearm sixteen (16) times, hits their intended target once, incapacitating the individual, as an *Objective Completion Rate* of 100%.

This new metric effectively obscures the reality that, as a general rule (from my experience as a Police Firearms Instructor in the NYPD), that officers discharged rounds make impact on their intended targets approximately 15% to 20% of the number of rounds fired during the confrontation.

Before there was SOP-9 some other means had to be found in order to mine the hard data necessary to make training and equipment decisions. Some examples are;

How did the FTS determine at what distances our firearms qualification courses should be laid out? Today, with the Federal Bureau of Investigation (FBI) annual police shooting reports, it is easy to see just what the actual combat distances between law officers and their adversaries are nationally. When the FTS first looked at the issue, the situation was more complex. Without computers, or the internet, Frank MaGee had to figure out what the *Practical* needs of the officers receiving training were. Before Frank, department members, in order to qualify with their handguns, were arrayed in front of bullseye targets with their six shot revolvers loaded with five rounds for each course fired. Using one hand, they'd fire a series of rounds just as a sport target shooter would; slow, timed and rapid fire, Why were only five rounds loaded in a handgun that held six? Because ammunition came in fifty round boxes, and it made for a neat series of training exercises ending with no extraneous rounds of ammunition left over.

Yet, officers were being found dead who had attempted to reload their still loaded handguns after firing five rounds, dumping a good live round on the ground in the process.

Frank knew that such training was abysmally useless as well as being downright dangerous, and he set about to prove it. He ordered members of the FTS to go to every precinct in the city (there are around eighty) and dig into the sometimes over one hundred year old Command Logs of each one of them, most buried deep in the basements of those old buildings. In those logs were contained not only the details of daily precinct life, but before computers (indeed, before typewriters!) every meaningful event that took place within the bounds of the precinct was documented within those large books. That included police deaths and shootings.

What Frank discovered was that we fought today just as we did in the mid-nineteenth century (the earliest references to police involved shootings that could be found), up close and personal. Historically, most of our combat had taken place at under twenty feet. Indeed, the vast majority of gunfights were within ten feet, the same as we see happening today! Yet, we were having our officers fire their handguns in both training and practice at twenty-five yards! This made no sense and he altered our training and qualification protocols accordingly.

Yet, even now, firearms instructors are having their students fire their handguns in training and qualification beyond fifteen yards. Why? Such distances are, for most shooters, neither practical nor task related.

When accepting a piece of equipment for testing we required that the vendor sign off on a receipt that read the item would be tested "to destruction." In truth, we rarely went that far with a piece of test gear, but with that proviso the vendor had no complaints should we damage their product during the testing process. And test we did. Before putting any equipment out in the field, the FTS would first attempt to place samples with the patrol force. Our reasoning was simple. Consider this, when we made an error, that error was multiplied over thirty thousand times! None the less, sometimes mistakes were made.

One example of the consequences of an undetected problem stands out in my mind. For a period of time department members were authorized to wear black leather jackets. Although the department members liked the jacket, the political hierarchy of the department became concerned over officer image, and decided a more benign look was appropriate. Thus, a modern, blue nylon insulated jacket was procured and put out on the street. What could possibly go wrong with that?

During this period reports started to come in from officers in the field indicating they were finding their revolvers (yes, it was a long time ago...) cocked in their holsters. Understand, during this time in the department's history, officers wore a very old holster design which had an open top, their revolvers being kept in place by an internal leather piece pushed aside by the shooters' thumb as they withdrew the handgun. Remarkably, few if any revolvers were ever snatched from our officers possession when this holster was in use.

Ranking members of the department, safe behind their bullet-proof desks, and seeing these reports of cocked handguns in holsters come in, dismissed them as somehow being the fault of the patrol officers nervously toying with their revolver's hammers. But the reports continued, and increased, from all parts of the city. Something was going on.

Well, the jackets had been put in service without any prior testing (issuing articles of clothing was the responsibility of the Equipment Section, not the FTS!). It turned out that the zipper tabs on the new jackets had a large hole in them. From time to time a tab would find itself atop the open holsters the officers wore and, on occasion, the hole in the tab would permit the revolver's hammer spur to enter and catch. When the officer jerked on his jacket, their revolver's hammer would sometimes become cocked!

The fix was to order thirty plus thousand little plastic snaps to go through the holes in the zipper tabs, as well as to make sure newly ordered jackets had modified zippers. The point of this story is, there was a reason the FTS found the thorough testing of equipment prior to its general issue to be so important. And why, as a firearms user or instructor, you should not be overly quick to adopt some newly introduced firearm or piece of equipment until such time as you can be assured that all the kinks have been worked out!

It's important for me to make clear that, while this book is designed for instructing in the fundamentals of handgun use, I urge those interested to locate whatever good quality additional training programs are out there, and take those which they can practically attend. There are many fine training schools around the nation. Do a bit of research and take advantage of the knowledge and skills these instructors can offer you. The more a person handles their firearms, the more muscle memory is retained by the shooter. There is rarely such a thing as too much training.

Richard P. Rosenthal
Chief of Police, Wellfleet MA, retired
Lieutenant, NYPD, retired

Five Fundamentals of Marksmanship

This is the book's first chapter because it's the most important. Mastering the fundamentals of marksmanship will ensure that the shooter will be able to operate his or her handguns as competently as possible. Indeed, it is virtually impossible to proceed to a higher level of proficiency unless the basics are understood, worked on and become second nature.

As you become more familiar with firearms, and hopefully seek competent professional training, you'll discover that there are variations on how to properly and efficiently use a handgun. I point this out to you for a number of reasons; I do not want you to believe that every suggestion found here is the best possible way to perform the tasks discussed, or is the best and only way for you to operate your handgun successfully. There are very experienced instructors who hold other views on the "right way" to do things. Some may well be correct, some perhaps not so correct. Other variables you ought to be aware of include the physical size of your hands, your body structure, eyesight limitations (personal ergonomic needs) and to what purpose you plan on putting the firearms you train with. Evaluate whatever training and information that comes before you with a critical mind and with the goal of enhancing your skills with a handgun. Indeed, every time I attend a training program, I come away with some information I either never knew before or had never thought of.

As this chapter discusses just what you need to know in order to execute and master the fundamentals of marksmanship I've included, when appropriate, an overview as to why each element is important and, to a limited degree, a brief history as to how our training has evolved over the years. While I trust that the material it contains is of interest to all readers, it's intended for both the beginning student as well as the firearms instructor and the seriously interested shooter.

*

The five fundamentals of marksmanship are:

➢ Sight picture
➢ Trigger control
➢ Proper grip
➢ Proper stance
➢ Breath control

We'll go over each one in detail;

Sight Picture

Sight Picture is defined as properly aligned sights in proper relation to their target.

Properly aligned sights mean, the front sight blade (your primary aiming point) is neither higher nor lower than the wings of the rear sight, with an equal amount of light separating the sides of the front sight with the wings of the rear sight.

Front sight is clear, rear sight and target is blurry

Note: the target, as well as the wings of the rear sight, are blurry to the eyes of the shooter. Only the front sight is sharp and in clear focus to the eyes. This is most important. Stop for a moment and consider this; when we discuss the standard sights of a handgun (front and rear sights) in relation to a target, we are speaking about *three separate objects*, each a different distance from the shooter's eye. <u>The human eye can only focus on a single object at any one moment in time.</u>

When using your handgun's sights, you must focus on the front sight! Your front sight is, indeed must be, your primary aiming point!

Except under close combat conditions (this is contact-distance, where your adversary is so close, they could possibly grab hold of your handgun) the front sight is what you will focus your eyes on. This is not debatable. It is common for people, during the excitement, terror and commotion of a gunfight, to miss a human size target at distances of five feet and even less!

At close range (contact to around ten feet), you must at least focus on the front sight. As range increases (from around ten feet to about twenty feet from your target), begin to use a "flash sight picture." That is, your front sight should be in rough alignment with the wings of your rear sight. As range increases (roughly ten yards and over), you'll need a solid sight picture with your sights properly aligned.

To reiterate the above;

> ➤ Close Combat/Contact Distance – no sights used, weapon held close to shooter's body to prevent weapon being snatched from them by an adversary.
> ➤ Just beyond arm's length, to around twenty feet – focus is on the front sight, placing the front sight in the center of the target's mass.
> ➤ Twenty feet to around ten yards – attempt to acquire a "flash" sight picture. The front sight remains the primary aim point, but the shooter should be conscious of the rear sight and its relation of the front sight and the target.
> ➤ Beyond ten yards – shooter should strive for a good sight picture, with properly aligned sights in proper relation to the intended target.

Importance of focusing on the front sight, particularly under combat conditions

It's not uncommon for a shooter to miss a human size target at a distance of five feet with a handgun unless the front sight is on the target. When a young detective working in the 14th Detective Division Robbery Squad (located in Brooklyn, New York) I recall going to the scene of a reported robbery-in-progress with shots fired within the 81 precinct. As with most robbery-in-progress calls, by the time the police got there the action had been over for some time. The location, a small liquor store situated in what can only be charitably described as a "high crime area" had been robbed by five young men, one armed with a .25 ACP caliber pistol. The proprietor, shaken up and leaning on the store's counter when I walked in, had been lawfully armed with a Smith and Wesson (S&W) model 60, a five round capacity .38 Special caliber revolver. There had been an exchange of shots at a distance of perhaps five feet (the distance across the top of the counter). The armed robber fired once, striking the proprietor in the calf of his leg. My victim required two Band-Aids (there was an entry and an exit wound) as well as a tetanus shot. He fired two rounds from his revolver at his assailants.

I asked him if he had hit anyone? He became agitated and angry, responding with a terse, "Of course I hit someone!" I then took a moment to look around. The place was quite small. All the bottles on the wall were intact, as was the glass windows and door. There were no holes in the floor either. I thought to myself, perhaps the man did strike one of the five robbers. I then looked up at the ceiling. He had made a nice two shot group…

Where did he go wrong? Five people, five feet away, how does one miss someone, anyone, at that distance? The answer is, he hadn't focused on his front sight, just grabbed his small handgun and, sticking it in front of his face, jerked off two rounds, the barrel pointed up at the ceiling.

Ed McGivern was an incredible exhibition shooter during the 1930s. He could fire, and empty, his S&W revolvers in a fraction of a second, putting all his rounds inside a playing card, hit targets tossed in the air with two guns firing at the same time, and hit marbles and dime size lead slugs consistently, also when tossed in the air. His feats were witnessed by many, many people as well as filmed and photographed. According to McGivern the handgun's front sight was used all the time for these incredible feats of marksmanship. He stated the following in regard the use of his handguns' sights:

"I had learned to use the sights quickly and accurately on moving targets ..."[1]

He also stated;

"That sights cannot be, and are not used, in this kind of shooting (rapid fire and aerial targets) is a radically wrong impression based entirely on theory and lack of actual knowledge of the subject."[2]

And,

"Any man who has developed any consistent shooting ability whatever can do better shooting with sights suitable for his particular kind of work than he can without them."[3]

When firing a handgun, not focusing on the front sight means it would be only a matter of chance and luck that you might strike your intended target.

*

Trigger Control

Slapping, yanking on or jerking a handgun's trigger will ensure a miss. A slap of the trigger at the end of the trigger pull, in an attempt to get the shot off when the sights are aligned with the target, will guarantee a miss and not be noticeable to the shooter due to the blast and recoil of the fired round. The reason for this is that the sudden, uncoordinated, pull of the trigger will bring the sights out of alignment and cause the round to go wide of the intended target. The problem is exacerbated as distance from the target increases due to the angular error created by the misalignment of the front and rear sights in relation to the target.

The goal, as former Border Patrol Agent Bill Jordan once wrote in his book, _No Second Place Winner_, was to, "Take your time ~ Fast!"[4] You can only get off rounds accurately in the amount of time you've trained your hand to operate your handgun's trigger properly and while under your control. This takes much repetitive practice in order to establish the proper muscle memory so as to permit the shooter control their handgun's trigger.

For the new shooter (and for many who have been around the range for a long time but never bothered to learn the basics of marksmanship) you should practice keeping the front sight on the target or, if at a greater distance, the sights aligned, while putting a slow and steady pressure on the handgun's trigger. Speed comes with practice. Bill Jordan's admonition, and your goal, to "Take your time ~ Fast!" is not to be taken lightly.

One technique I've used to train my students when teaching the operation of the double-action (self-cocking) revolver, is to place (base down) a live round upon the handgun's top strap. Extend the handgun out to arm's length and slowly squeeze the trigger without causing the round to fall off the handgun. It takes practice, but once mastered goes a long way in teaching oneself how to control a handgun's trigger.

Semi-auto handguns, at least the very popular "safety action" variety, are somewhat problematic when wishing to engage in such an exercise in that they require the slide to be brought to the rear and released in order to set the trigger, making this type of practice impractical when done alone. You need to have a helper who can rack the slide back to reset the trigger and assist you in your practice session.

One last word in regard engaging in the above mentioned training exercise. Be very, very careful to ensure that you have fully, and properly, unloaded your handgun prior to this type of practice. Trust me on this, check the firearm's chamber/s at least twice and make sure all ammunition is someplace else prior to initiating this training exercise.

*

I believe a note on the different types of actions most commonly encountered in modern handguns would be appropriate here. The colloquial terms describing them that I've heard most frequently in use are;

- ➢ Single-action
- ➢ Double-action (Self-cocking)
- ➢ Safety action

Single-action handguns may be found in both revolvers and semi-automatic pistols. The single-action revolver was first popularized with Colt's 1836 Patterson revolver, so you can see that the design goes back quite a while. Another example of the type is the venerable Colt .45 "Peacemaker" (1873). With this style mechanism the shooter must first manually (using the thumb) bring the hammer of the revolver back to full cock. A short and relatively light pull of the trigger permits the hammer to fall, discharging the piece.

This revolver design is usually found in sporting handguns and is used extensively in cowboy action shoots.

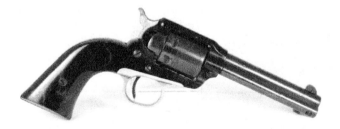

A Single-Action Ruger Bearcat .22 Revolver

An example of the hammer-fired single-action pistol (semi-automatic handgun) is the Colt 1911A1. The 1911 pistol's hammer may be either brought to full cock by the shooter's thumb or, when the slide is brought to the rear to load the piece, the hammer comes back and remains in the full cock position. This action type is still quite popular, including among some police and military units. It does require a significant amount of training (and the development of well-established muscle memory) before it should be considered to be used for "serious purposes."

Some of the first successful striker-fired (hammerless) single-action handguns were the 1893 Borchardt, Luger of 1900, Colt's .25 ACP of 1908 and the Savage model of 1910 as well as a number of other pocket pistols from that period. Striker fired handguns come in several variations. Older types were, most generally, single-action only. That is, each round was fired by a relatively short, light pull on the pistol trigger.

Glock 19, 9x19mm Safety Action pistol with light attached

A newer design is that of the striker-fired, "double-action only" (some called "safety-action") pistols. In this type of mechanism each round

8

fired is accomplished with a fairly long pull on the handgun trigger, similar in feel and action to that of the double-action revolver.

A Sig 220 is a DA to SA type pistol

Some semi-auto pistols, such as the Sig 220 shown, may be fired by first pulling on the trigger for the first round. This discharges the piece, cycling the action, which cocks the exposed hammer and permits such handguns to be fired single-action for subsequent rounds (hammer to the rear, with a light and short trigger pull).

The double-action revolver (such handguns are more accurately referred to as self-cockers, an arcane term no one but the occasional firearms instructor ever seems to use) may be fired by simply pulling on the trigger. This causes the hammer to move to the rear, revolves and locks the cylinder and, at some point in the trigger stroke, permits the hammer to fall forward so as to discharge the handgun.

This is a very practical design, suitable for many purposes. There are variations among the manufacturers designs resulting in variations as to how much control a shooter may have over the accuracy potential of the handgun while firing them double-action. I've always been most comfortable with the feel of either the S&W or Ruger double-action trigger. While I own and have carried Colt revolvers (and they are fine handguns) I found them to be less suited for very accurate double-action work. Just my opinion.

A S&W DA revolver, the model 10

Should anyone try and persuade you that firing a handgun accurately is not possible using the double-action mechanism I again defer to that master handgun shot, Ed McGivern, who wrote, in regard to hitting marbles thrown in the air, "I had learned to use the sights quickly and accurately on moving targets (*McGivern is referring to thrown marbles!*) and **had learned to squeeze and control the trigger properly while also keeping the movements of the revolver under perfect control,…**"[5]

*

Your handgun must be gripped with sufficient firmness, and in a manner that is adequately secure, to aid in the aiming, manipulating and discharging the piece, but not to the point of causing tremor. New shooters don't consider the fact that when first firing handguns they are using an assortment of muscles in a heretofore unique combination. It takes some time for these muscles to develop strength and to "learn" to function smoothly together. After a day's firing at the practice range new shooters should not be surprised if their hand/s feel a bit sore, perhaps even cramped. Practice and time are the remedies.

Double-Action Revolver Combat Grip:

- ➢ Thumb is held low while putting pressure on the handgun's side plate (but not to the point of tremor).
- ➢ Trigger finger goes deep into the trigger guard.
- ➢ Pinky may go under the butt if comfortable and practical (if shooter's hand is large enough and the grip design will so allow), which will help reduce upward movement of the muzzle.
- ➢ The weak (support) hand grasps the shooting hand firmly (but not to the point of tremor).
- ➢ Weak (support) hand thumb locks onto and over the strong hand thumb.

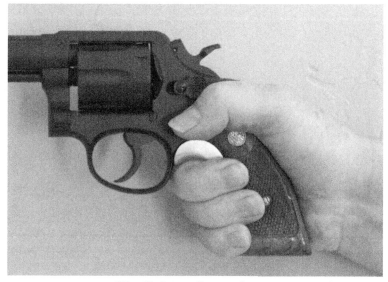

The DA revolver grip

11

Why do I suggest it's best, when using two hands, to lock "thumb to thumb" vs. digging the support hand thumb into the "V" (between the thumb and forefinger) of the strong shooting hand? Two reasons; There is more physical contact between the hands when done this way, and, when transitioning over to the semi-auto handgun the shooter's thumb will automatically be away from the sharp edged slide which cycles rapidly to the rear of the pistol after each round is fired. To leave your thumb behind the slide of a semi-auto pistol is to virtually ensure a nasty cut.

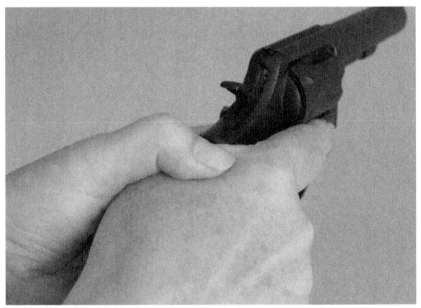

POOR GRIP TECHNIQUE! DON'T DIG YOUR SUPPORT HAND THUMB INTO THE WEB OF YOUR SHOOTING HAND!!

A word on "tea cupping." Some folks think they are accomplishing something positive when they place the shooting hand in the open palm of the non-shooting hand. This is referred to as "tea cupping" and serves no purpose, as the firearm, upon discharge, bounces merrily off the non-shooting hand.

Target Grip:

The single-hand target grip is quite different from the combat grip as it is, obviously, intended for a different purpose:

> ➢ Strong hand thumb is held high.
> ➢ Pad of trigger finger rests on trigger.
> ➢ Shooter's grip is somewhat "loose."

This is for the sporting (mostly formal target range) use of the handgun. Fine for its purpose but not all that relevant to the purpose of this book. At any rate I thought it prudent to at least mention it.

This is "tea-cupping." Don't do it!

*

Semi-automatic Pistol

Combat grip:

> ➢ Thumb is generally held just alongside and below the pistol's slide, clear of the mechanism's controls, while putting pressure on the handgun's side (not to the point of tremor).*
> ➢ Pad of the trigger finger is placed on the trigger.

> ➤ The weak (support) hand grasps the shooting hand firmly (but not to the point of tremor).
> ➤ Weak (support) hand thumb locks onto strong hand thumb (some instructors prefer to teach both thumbs "point" in the same direction, one under the other).

Where the shooter's thumb is placed when firing a semi-auto pistol will vary with the model pistol. For example, with the 1911 type handgun, with its thumb safety situated by the end of the pistol's slide, we see many competent shooters who place their thumb above this model pistol's safety, to preclude inadvertently bumping the safety "up" and on.

Proper pistol grip

*

With whatever type action handgun you are shooting, unless there is a physical (or individual ergonomic) reason preventing it, ensure that the barrel, or top of the slide, is in line with your strong side forearm.

When training students in the proper technique to grip the handgun, I tend to be flexible. Modifications to a shooter's grip will depend on a number of variables; among them being the size of the hand, length of the fingers and student's hand strength. Please treat the above grip recommendations as a guide.

*

Just a note on the human hand and the proper ergonomic design of a handgun's grip. As you see from the photo below, the human hand, in its natural position, is wider at the top and more narrow at the bottom. My point is, avoid handgun grips where the bottom of the grip is flared out. Such a design is the exact opposite of what is required for a good, solid, handgun grip. It's one reason why so many revolver shooters like to install a grip-adapter (or spacer), such as the Tyler-T or BK grip adapter, on their factory stock grips. Such adapters take up the dead-space behind the trigger guard, making for a superior grip for the shooter.

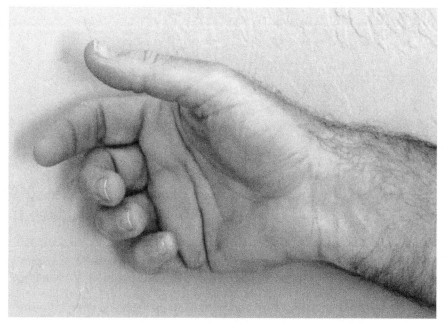

***The human hand, when closing, is wider at the top
than at the bottom***

*

Stance

There are two primary shooting stances, isosceles or Weaver (developed by Jack Weaver in 1959, then a Los Angeles Deputy Sheriff and competitive handgun shooter). These stances have been further modified by several professional firearms instructors. Your choice of stance will depend on your goals as a firearms user as well as how comfortable and natural you find each of the kinds of shooting stances you will be introduced to.

*

Combat Stances (either isosceles or Weaver stance – Shooter's choice)

Isosceles Stance:

> ➤ Legs shoulder width apart.
> ➤ Weak side leg may be a bit forward, or otherwise as most natural for the individual.
> ➤ Some crouching of the body is permissible.
> ➤ Lock all arm joints!
>   (wrist, elbows, shoulder)
> ➤ Push/pull with arms (push out with the shooting arm, pull in with the weak side arm).
> ➤ Keep head up. Don't "scrunch" your head down to the line of sight.

Weaver Stance:

> ➤ Basically, the position takes on that of the "interrogation" or "fighter's" stance. That is, the shooter is partially "bladed" in relation to the target.
> ➤ Weapon comes up from the ready position with the sights aligned.
> ➤ Keep head up. Don't "scrunch" your head down to the line of sight.
> ➤ Suitable for all handgun types.

> ➤ Permits easy fluid movement.
> ➤ If used by a law officer the officer must ensure the bullet resistant vest they wear covers the sides of the body.

Please note, any position taken may be modified to adapt to the ergonomic needs of the shooter.

The locking of the various flexible parts of the arm warrants further discussion. Every non-locked joint within the extended arm decreases the accuracy potential of the shooter. Furthermore, the wrist is made up of many small bones (thirteen bones and four joints). Good solid and deliberate control of the wrists joints and muscles is important to the accurate firing of a handgun.

*

Target Stance

For the "record" I've opted to include the target (sporting) stance in the book:

> ➤ Shooter stands 45 degrees to target.
> ➤ The non-shooting hand is immobilized (generally placed in the pocket).
> ➤ Handgun, unsupported, is raised to eye level.
> ➤ Proper sight picture is obtained and is extremely important in this exercise.

Note: Shooters should close their eyes while the handgun is held on the target downrange. They should then open their eyes and observe if the sights are still on the target. If off target (left or right of target), shooters should alter their stance by moving the rear leg left or right, in order to bring the handgun's sights back on target. Repeat as necessary. Doing this avoids "fighting" one's own body muscle structure when aiming the sidearm. The goal is to acquire your natural point of aim using this technique. I remind you that this stance is for the sporting use of the handgun.

Ready Position:

There are times when it is either necessary to move about while the handgun remains held in one's hands or, if stationary, when it is desirable for the handgun to be out of its holster yet ready for immediate firing. One ready position is called the "low-ready," another is the "high-ready."

With the low-ready the shooter's arms and firearm are held at about a 45 degree angle to the ground, trigger finger alongside, above –and out of!– the trigger guard. To engage a target all the shooter need do is bring the firearm up to eye level, focus on the front sight (or secure a full sight picture, as appropriate to the distance to the target), while at the same moment placing the trigger finger on the trigger. This ready position is often used at training facility ranges in lieu of having the shooters fire their pistols after drawing from their holsters.

The high-ready position has the gun held up at about chest height.

Working from either of the two ready positions ensures a number of positives for the shooter;

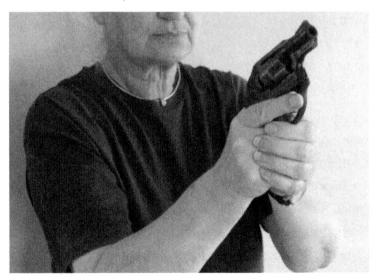

High Ready

Low Ready

> ➤ There is less tendency to bring the gun up past (above and beyond) the shooter's line of sight. This habit blocks the shooter's view of the target, often at a critical moment.
> ➤ There is also less likelihood that the shooter will push out with the firearm, which generally causes shots to go low.
> ➤ More mobility is afforded the shooter. The shooter can comfortably move about, safely for himself and others, yet have a firearm immediately ready for use.

Unsupported:

Firing the handgun with only one hand should be practiced regularly, if only for those rare occasions when you are doing something very, very important with your non-shooting hand and cannot have a two handed grip on your firearm (if a law officer this might mean; holding on to a prisoner, using a flashlight, holding something really, really important in the weak hand [a portable radio?] or if the weak hand is disabled).

Retired Marine Corps Major Jim Land –at one time Jim was responsible for Marine Corp firearms training– once said to me; "When shooting, not only do I use both of my hands on my pistol, but, if I could, I'd get both of my feet on top as well!" If Jim Land tells you to do something, I suggest you heed his words!

For safety, during this type of training immobilize the weak hand across the chest. Firmly lock all the joints of the shooting arm. You'll find that when using only one hand instead of two-handed supported shooting, you'll see a profound difference in both practical accuracy as well as the speed with which you can get off your rounds.

Hip shooting:

Shooting from the hip (not "point-shooting," where the handgun is held chest high by the shooter), while appearing sophisticated to the uninitiated, is, in point of fact, of little practical value. I'm not speaking of close combat shooting techniques (contact close or close quarter combat), where the sidearm is held in tight against the body in order to prevent a close-in assailant (a person within arm's reach) the ability to grab your handgun. Hip shooting is the style of firing the weapon where, for some reason the shooter believes that discharging the handgun with the front sight several inches below the line of sight is somehow superior to raising the handgun up the required distance (perhaps twelve to eighteen inches, taking a micro-second of time to accomplish) in order to place the front sight on target and actually ensure a hit.

Shooters will sometimes play at hip shooting, "walking" shots on paper until the rounds impact where they desire. This is fine, unless there is no paper target in front of them on which to walk the rounds! Unless a person is prepared to develop very specialized muscle memory to hit a target without first seeing where the rounds are going, I submit the exercise serves no valid purpose.

There is always time to at least use the front sight unless under close combat conditions (arm's length distance). We'll discuss close combat shooting in a moment.

The above comments do not mean I am unaware that some folks have trained themselves to be very accurate shots while shooting from the hip. Indeed, there are exhibition shooters that can hit an aspirin from the hip at twenty feet. If you wish to teach yourself that skill, that's fine. The ability to regularly hit an intended target from the hip will require a great deal of training to master, as well as continued practice to maintain. My goal here is the practical application of the handgun, thus this type of shooting technique serves no useful purpose for further discussion in this book.

*

Breath Control/Respiratory Pause

For practical combat shooting purposes this is the least important element of the five fundamentals of marksmanship.

During the respiratory pause, there is a natural cessation of air intake of about ten seconds, at which time the shooter should endeavor to get off the shot. If the shooter waits too long and continues to withhold air intake into the lungs a tremble will be induced, the shooter's eyes will water, and the body will (involuntarily) direct the shooter to get the shot off so that it can once again breath!

For target shooting as well as in rifle shooting breath control is important. With the rifle especially, breath control is used to adjust and fine tune the point of aim of the telescopic sight's reticule.

*

Master Eye/Dominant Eye Check

The shooter must know which eye is the master or dominant eye. It is important to determine whether the shooter's master eye and strong side hand are on the same side. If this is not the case the shooter will need to modify both grip and stance accordingly. Some instructors believe the master eye so important that the shooter might be better to shoot using the hand located on the same side as of that individual's master eye.

Make a "hole" using both hands (or make a "circle" with your thumb and index fingers, or cut a hole in a piece of paper). View some distant object through the hole, using both eyes (both eyes remain open during this exercise). The shooter should bring the "hole" to their eye without losing sight of the object. Whichever eye the hole winds up in front of is the shooter's master eye.

*

Random Relevant Notes:

When shooting at objects which are very close (as when dispatching an injured animal) it must be remembered that the handgun's projectile will impact well under the tip of the front sight at such close distances. It would prove a useful learning experience if the shooter would take a piece of blank paper, draw a walnut size circle in its middle (about the size of a raccoon's brain), and at a distance of three feet attempt to hit that target. The shooter will observe that in order to hit that object will require the top of the front sight to be approximately one inch above the actual target.

This is why police officers tend to do such a terrible job when dispatching small animals and deer which are found lying injured on the road. The officer's projectiles are badly missing their intended target, leaving the officer to wonder at the practical utility of their sidearms as a tool for personal defense.

*

Should you need to shoot from cover, as in behind some sort of a barricade, use a conventional hold regardless of the side of the barricade you find yourself. Your weapon may have to be held at an angle in order to do so comfortably. That's fine.

Avoid "speed" reholstering. Getting your handgun safely and securely from your holster is laudable, and a necessary task to master. Once the firing is over there is little need to be in a hurry to put your handgun back in the holster. Take your time when reholstering. There is rarely an ongoing emergency that requires speed in order to relieve yourself of having to have a pistol in your hand.

*

Common Problems

This is the "catch-all" part of the chapter, where I put in issues I couldn't figure out how to shoehorn in someplace else. We'll take them one at a time:

After a poorly aimed shot – commenting, remarking or shaking one's head (in disgust?) after that last round is fired.

FORGET ABOUT THE LAST SHOT YOU JUST FIRED!!

I really mean that last admonition;
~FORGET ABOUT THE LAST SHOT YOU JUST FIRED!!~

I was taught this many years ago by a very experienced police firearms instructor, a former national NRA police revolver champion, and a really nice guy. I met Officer Frank May around 1972 or 1973, when taking advantage of the New York City Police (NYPD) department's permitting each officer fifty rounds of practice ammo a month, to be fired at any of the half dozen or so in-door ranges used during the winter shooting cycle. I'd go to two or three different indoor department ranges a month to take advantage of this "perk."

Frank was the firearms instructor assigned to the indoor range in Staten Island. When he saw that I was intensely interested in improving my shooting skills he began to mentor me, teaching me the proper double-action technique for accurate shooting with my S&W model 10.

Back then we practiced a good deal of the time firing the revolver at a distance of twenty-five yards at bullseye targets, shooting three, ten-round strings of slow, timed and rapid fire. All firing was done using the revolver's double-action mechanism only.

While firing one string of rapid fire I discharged my piece and thought I'd blown a shot. I shook my head, uttered the word "shit!" and continued firing the remainder of the rounds in the cylinder. Sure enough, one of my shots was out of the bull and in the nine ring.

When finished, I removed my hearing protection. Frank, standing behind me, calmly commented (and I'm paraphrasing here), "The round where you shook your head and cursed, that was in the bullseye. Your next shot was the one you threw in the nine ring."

That lesson Frank taught me nearly fifty years ago has stayed with me. I've shared this instruction with hundreds of shooters. A few may have actually listened. The last round you've fired is gone. There is nothing more you can do about it. It's history. Concentrate on the next shot coming up. There is no other option.

Permit me one off-topic Frankie May story. It was a Friday, meaning it was Frank's last day at work that week until the coming Monday. When I came in to shoot my fifty rounds, I noticed that Frank had his model 10 completely disassembled, and was methodically cleaning the revolver. Sometime later, after he had put the revolver back together, I watched as he took his hearing protection, eye protection, the revolver and six rounds of ammunition off his desk and walked over to the range only a few feet away. He loaded the gun and fired the six rounds downrange.

I laughed and made fun of him going through all that trouble of cleaning his sidearm, only to fire six rounds moments later. Frank replied, "I just had the gun completely apart. I wanted to make sure I hadn't screwed (he actually used a stronger word) anything up."

Thinking back about his words, and now with more than a few years of experience under my belt, I must agree with Frank's philosophy. When

I thoroughly clean any of my handguns, particularly if it's a semi-auto pistol, I'm not happy until I fire a magazine of ammo downrange through the newly cleaned handgun, just to make sure I hadn't "screwed anything up."

*

Looking at the target OVER the sights of the handgun.

To the instructor this act is very obvious. Some students, regardless of the number of times I, as their instructor, directed them not to change focus from the front sight to the target during the time it took them to finish the shooting exercise, completely ignored me. The shooters will fire a round then, while keeping the firearm extended and pointed downrange, raise their head to view their handiwork on the target downrange. In short, in so doing these shooters are defeating the purpose of focusing on their front sight.

So long as you are engaging your target, that is, firing on your target or about to fire on your target, your aiming point must be your front sight. At least if you have any intent on hitting what you are aiming at.

*

Permitting the elbows and wrist to unlock.

The less rigid the joints of the arm are, the greater will be the dispersion of the rounds fired. As with all else involved in the handling of firearms, it requires repetition, and practice, for a person to automatically lock their joints when bringing their firearm up to eye level.

*

Raising the handgun above the target then bringing it back down to target level.

Stated differently, the shooter brings the handgun up to, past and beyond eye/target level. It's nothing more than an unfortunate habit and should be broken by the instructor as soon as it is first observed. Nothing positive is accomplished by this action. As the firearm comes up to, and beyond, eye/target level, whatever lays before the shooter's view is blocked by the shooter's own hands and handgun.

*

Scrunching shooter's head down and to one side when in a shooting stance.

This is done by many shooters, including, as I have observed, some superb shots, so I have to tread lightly here. It will be to the shooter's advantage if, when taking a shooting stance, they keep the head relatively level, and both eyes on the same plane.

All you accomplish when forcing the head down (and to the side) in an exaggerated manner is to put a great deal of muscle pressure, strain and tension, on the muscles of the neck, for no gain.

Spend some time on YouTube and search out videos of master handgun shots. One could do worse than to emulate their stances and styles of shooting.

*

Much of the initial training I do with new students is at quite close range. My personal favorite is a fifty round drill called a Ball and Dummy exercise. It's easiest done with the revolver, but it is also possible to accomplish with the semi-auto pistol (dummy rounds are needed with the semi-auto).

Whether with a revolver or semi-auto pistol, a large blank target (just turn a training target around to the blank side) is affixed to the target backing. The student(s) is told to stand between ten and twenty feet from the target. Each is given a box of ammunition, generally fifty rounds.

If armed with a revolver, the shooters are directed to fully load their handguns. They are instructed that speed is neither of value nor desired in this exercise, that the goal is to ensure that the students are focusing on their front sights and controlling their triggers.

From the ready position the students are commanded to raise their handguns to eye level and s-l-o-w-l-y fire six rounds. The instructor will at that point have some idea who his problem shooters are and who his "star" pupils are.

Students are then directed to remove three of the spent cartridges from their revolvers chambers and insert live rounds in their place, then give the cylinder a light spin and close it. The order to fire is then given again, with the instructor carefully observing the trigger control of the students. The important pulls of the trigger are when there is an empty chamber under the hammer. A wag of the barrel, depending on direction of travel, will tell the instructor that the student is either yanking, pulling or jerking on the trigger.

The semi-auto needs to be handled in a different manner. The students should be instructed to load a number of magazines, alternating with several live rounds and an occasional plastic dummy round (cheaply available). So, when it's time for them to commence the exercise, the students will not only be learning to control their triggers and focus on their front sights, but they will engage in numerous failure-to-fire clearance drills as well ("tap, rack, bang" or, sometimes also referred to as "tap, rack, ready.").

*

Except for advanced training I hold that there is little to gain by moving the beginning firearms student much beyond ten to fifteen yards from their targets. Indeed, a good argument can be made that most journeyman level police officers would do well to routinely have their training limited to remaining as those distances from their training targets.

I found the following data from the NYPD Firearms Discharge Report (formerly SOP-9) from 2010. It shows that 89% of the gunfight distances that year were under twenty feet! This is normal. This is what has been observed ever since data has been recorded on the subject. The reason is pretty simple. How people engage in combat with one another has not changed over the years.

Muggers don't rob their victims from across the street. Purse snatchers have to get up close and personal to do their deed. Officers interact with citizens as a matter of routine from a distance well within arm's reach. And should something untoward take place, such as when a routine interview turns into a conversation with a wanted, armed felon, the event happens very quickly and very close.

NYPD data from SOP-9 ~ 2010 ~ Gunfight Distances by Percent

0~5'	26%
6~10'	39%
11~15'	8%
16~20'	16%

89% of confrontations were at 20' or less!

21~50'	11%
+50'	1 round fired

*

Here is one real life example:

New York City Saturday, April 7th, 2012, 61 pct. Brooklyn

Police responded Saturday night to a report of a man with a gun...

Receiving no response, they concluded that the woman and child were being held hostage and summoned Emergency Service Officers and hostage negotiators. An ESU and hostage negotiation team arrived and were in the process of taking up positions outside of the apartment when the woman suddenly opened the door and fled the apartment with the baby in her arms.

She told the officers that Foxworth had been holding her hostage and was armed. As the six-man Emergency Service team entered, they were immediately fired upon by Foxworth. He had emerged from a bedroom, firing a nine-millimeter Browning semi-automatic.

He fired 12 times striking Detective Michael Keenan in his left calf, Detective Kenneth Ayala in the thigh and foot and Police Officer Matthew Granahan in his left calf. Captain Al Pizzano also sustained a graze wound to his face.

The gunfight occurred in close quarters, with **the assailant and the officers no more than 10 feet apart.** Although hit, Detective Ayala and Officer Granahan returned fire striking Foxworth in the abdomen.

*

The handgun is a difficult weapon to shoot accurately. The theoretical accuracy (the accuracy of a good quality firearm firing high quality ammunition) is actually quite good – with accurate ammunition, from a machine rest, a plain vanilla police service revolver may well group its rounds into about a 1.5" circle at 25 yards. Yet, when we see these same handguns at the firing range, that accuracy potential is rarely matched.

The reasons are fairly obvious. Practical handgun accuracy –particularly when the shooter is under stress– is much worse than what these firearms are capable of. The inhibiting factors are many:

> ➤ Handguns are light in weight yet their trigger pulls are relatively heavy. A twelve to forty-ounce handgun may have from four to sixteen-pound trigger pull.
> ➤ The blast, flash and recoil of service ammunition are all inhibiting factors in regard the practical accuracy of handguns.

Fortunately, at least in regard the practical accuracy of handguns, most encounters requiring the need for a sidearm are at very close range –the vast majority of the incidents taking place less than twenty feet from the shooter. Simply stated, this is how humans engage in combat with one another. And a gun fight is, fundamentally, hand to hand combat.

With proper training in the practical (combat) use of the handgun, hits on human size targets can be readily attained. To accomplish this, training must be structured so that, within reason and safety limits, the training process duplicates combat conditions to the degree it is reasonable and safely possible to do so.

Experience has demonstrated that during periods of stress trained individuals will respond as they were trained. Failing to properly train individuals will likely result in panic, or perhaps more accurately, the individuals will simply not know what to do, when faced with an armed assailant. At that point it is impossible to foretell what their actions will be during such a high stress situation.

Furthermore, if a person is trained to do the wrong thing that is what they will do when under stress.

*

Some History and Old Training Techniques

For many many years handgun training was based on custom, aesthetics, assumed truths, and for the convenience of those conducting the instruction. Handguns were fired offhand, held only in the shooters strong hand, unsupported by the weak hand. I know of at least one state police agency that required both left handed as well as right handed troopers to carry their sidearms on the right hand side of the body. It gave a more uniform appearance to the unit's members and simply looked better.

Officers were once taught to fire their six round revolvers with five round strings of fire. This was because boxes of ammo came in fifty round units and made life easier for the instructors.

In order to simplify clean-up, immediately after firing brass would routinely be dumped in a "brass can" (empty coffee can), or were caught in shooters hands, with shooters then placing the rounds in their pockets. On occasion, officers would be found dead or wounded with empty brass in their pockets. How you train is how you will react.

The cocking of the handgun (single-action mode) was routinely done during firing exercises. This lead to officers cocking their guns in the field when anticipating trouble. Aside from the fact that a quality revolver is no more accurate fired single-action then when fired double-action, and is much slower to get off repeat shots as well, this habit also led to many accidental discharges and unintentional injuries to both officers and citizens.

It was not that long ago that bullseye targets were the norm instead of the now ubiquitous combat silhouettes. Never having seen a large black dot pasted on a bad guy's torso, it makes one wonder what the people in charge of firearms training were thinking at the time.

Not everyone in the field of firearms training were so rigid in their beliefs. Colonel Rex Applegate, an American military officer who served during World War II with the forerunner of the Central Intelligence Agency, the Office of Strategic Services, came to understand the limitations of handgun training protocols of the day. He eventually realized, through empirical observation, that highly skilled bullseye shooters were terribly ineffective when using their sidearms under even low stress, close combat situations. He demonstrated that expert shots (as rated by the standards of the day) would miss silhouette size targets consistently, at distances no greater than ten feet!

Colonel Applegate, when assigned to train a specialized group within the Army, developed an interesting, practical and effective program for training large numbers of individuals in close range combat shooting. Applegate created what he referred to as a "House of Horrors." The shooting range was located within a building. Its internal design was created to throw shooters off balance, build up tension as they went through the course of fire, and increase their hit potential when engaging varying targets under unexpected circumstances.

Applegate would have his shooters enter one at a time. An instructor, in physical contact with the shooter at all times, was also present. Lighting was kept dim, string dangled from the ceilings to simulate cobwebs. Targets were of the silhouette type, some stationary, some "popped down" or moved into view when the instructor pulled on a string.

Shooters were armed with an assortment of firearms, ranging from military service handguns in .45 ACP and .38 Special calibers as well as a .22 long rifle version of the Colt service pistol. Recordings, both of eerie music as well as screams and "torture scenes" played loudly. There were twelve targets to be engaged, two times each.

After the first five hundred men went through the program, all either marksman or expert rated shooters, Applegate evaluated their success and found that out of the twelve rounds fired, those shooters averaged only four hits each. And not one of the targets was further than ten feet from the shooters![6]

Next time you see in the news a story about a police officer missing an armed adversary at fairly close range, keep Colonel Applegate's House of Horrors in mind.

*

Types of Range Operation:

There are, generally speaking, two ways to run a firearms range; Hot Range and Cold Range. With a Hot Range the firearm is always loaded and is either holstered or at the ready position and about to engage the target(s).

A Hot Range requires the following:

> Weapons always loaded, either holstered, at the ready position, or engaging a target.

➢ Requires good discipline and attentive instructors.

➢ If there is a malfunction on the line – the students keep their handguns pointed downrange while they raise their non-shooting hand above their head.

➢ Clear, concise line commands are used. Each command repeated at least twice.

➢ The command "Cease Fire!" causes an immediate cessation to the firing. This command ends any exercise engaged in. This rule is important from a safety standpoint.

➢ The line is always called "Clear!" before shooters go downrange.

➢ No weapons are handled, or otherwise permitted out of their holsters, when shooters are downrange.

*

I have one last thought. All too often I've seen people involved in the shooting sports firing round after round, hitting their intended targets mostly by chance. At such times I silently wonder to myself if these folks aren't somehow involved in some clandestine ammunition disposal unit.

Mastering the sidearm takes time and practice. There are no shortcuts. Working at mastering the sidearm cannot be replaced or substituted with good equipment alone. You don't need the fanciest, newest, most gee-whiz gun that's come on the market in order to be a competent and successful shot. A good, solid, serviceable handgun, fired many times in practice, under the tutelage of a qualified and competent instructor, is the way to success in this endeavor.

The Fundamentals References

[1]McGivern, Ed, *Fast and Fancy Revolver Shooting*, Follett publishing, 1938, p.39

[2]*Ibid*, p. 43

[3]*Ibid*, p. 396

[4]Jordan, Bill, *No Second Place Winner,* © 1965 by W. H. Jordan, Shreveport, La, p. 107

[5]McGivern, Ed, *Fast and Fancy Revolver Shooting*, Follett publishing, 1938, p. 40.

[6]Applegate, Colonel Rex, *Crowd and Riot Control* (a revision of *Kill or get Killed*), the Stackpole Company, Harrisburg, PA, 1964, pgs. 383, 384.

Optical Red-Dot Sights

Until quite recently (approximately twenty years for military applications, perhaps less than a decade for law enforcement use), only "iron" sights (open-sights, mostly constructed of aluminum, plastic or steel) have been the sighting system utilized for the majority of handguns.

During this period, military, and now police agencies, have slowly come to realize the advantages offered users by the employment of optical, Micro Red-Dot Sights (MRDS).

As seen in the chapter on the fundamentals of marksmanship, open sights require the user to align both the front and rear sights of the handgun in a very specific manner, then position the now properly aligned sights on the target prior to firing the firearm. MRDS greatly simplify the process of aiming, by using only a single point of light (most often a dot, but there are variations) which is placed on the target, while both the dot, and the target, are in focus to the shooter's eyes.

What is a Micro Red-Dot Sight?

A MRDS is a small (weighing in at about one ounce), battery powered electric optical sight utilizing a light emitting diode (LED), with (most frequently) a small dot being projected onto a clear glass or plastic lens (part of the sight), which is the user's aiming point. A red-dot (generally the dot used is red, but some optical units use a green dot, others a triangle, some a circle, which may be of either color) is seen by the user, and these sights permit both the sight's red-dot, as well as the target, to be in clear focus to the shooter while aiming as well as at the moment of handgun discharge.

Sometimes these small (micro size) optical sights are used on long arms, but their size makes them most suitable for handguns. Red-dot sights have been around for approximately forty years or so (since the 1970s), but they have only, relatively recently, become miniaturized, and of suitable durability, to the point where they are practical for use on general issue law enforcement (and military) service size handguns, including models suitable for smaller pistols often carried by soft-clothes investigators, as well as by non-law enforcement affiliated citizens for personal defense.

Leupold Delta Point Pro–Battery is Replaced from the Top

The reason both the red-dot and the target are in focus at the same time is, in simple terms, because the dot is projected onto the lens, and then reflected back to the shooters eye, putting the dot and the target on the same focal plan. In effect, the image of the dot is viewed as being at infinity.

A further advantage of this type of sight is, these units possess virtually no "parallax." Parallax is the movement of the aiming point (the aiming dot in this case) in relation to the target as the shooter's eyes move behind and around the sight.

Richard P. Rosenthal

Dot size is measured in minute of angle (MOA). Roughly, one (1) MOA is equivalent to a one inch (1") circle at one hundred yards. For general purpose use, MRDS utilize any one of a number of different dot sizes. Many shooters, using these sights for personal defense, or for law enforcement applications, prefer a somewhat larger dot, generally six (6) to eight (8) MOA in size. Such preferences comes down to personal taste, as well as what application the handgun will be put to. For example, the author uses a three (3) MOA size dot for my sporting handguns, and a six (6) MOA dot for my handguns used for personal defense.

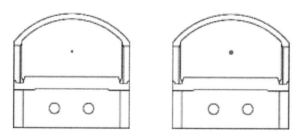

Representation a 3 MOA and 6 MOA Dot

Iron-Sights

Iron-sights (open sights) have been around for approximately five hundred years, evolving from crude variations of front-sights on the muzzle end of long arms, then on to assorted front-sights mated with groves cut into in the tops of the hammer of percussion revolvers, to today's sophisticated array of plastic, metal, tritium powered (self- illuminating), and fluorescent front-sights, matched with an assortment of rear-sight options, both fixed and adjustable.

Regardless of the type of open (iron-sights) used, they all suffer from the same liability, which is, requiring shooters to observe three distinct objects, each a different distance from the shooter's eyes. Shooters are trained to, for the most part (except during close combat situations), to focus on their handgun's front-sight. Once that is done, objects beyond the front-sight of their sidearm are indistinct, because, as stated earlier, the human eye cannot focus on more than one object at a time.

A simple experiment, to validate the above statement, would be for the reader to extend their forefinger out, in front of their face, at arm's length, and focus on their finger's tip, while at the same time observing which objects beyond that point appear well-defined in their line of vision. If the experiment is conducted with both eyes open (as is the desired method of aiming taught shooters), then the objects beyond the reader's fingertip will not only be blurry, but, with both eyes open, there will be two of them.

Indeed, when I wear my everyday bi-focal glasses, I cannot clearly see the front sight of a pistol (the sight is quite blurry). For shooting, I must wear my shooting glasses. It's for that reason I've put a MRDS on my everyday carry pistol. Now, with normal glasses, I can clearly see both the aiming point (the red-dot) as well as my intended target.

The human eye can only focus on one object at the same time. This is the heart of the dilemma shooters face when using iron-sights. If we do as we are trained, which is to focus on our front sights, all objects beyond the front sight will be indistinct (the degree of distortion will be dictated by the shooter's distance to the target).

Furthermore, to ensure accuracy, shooters are required to keep the post of the front sight neither higher nor lower than the top "wings" of their handgun's rear sight, with an equal amount of light showing on either side of the front sight. This is a skill which takes a great deal of practice to master.

Study Done on Relative Efficacy Comparing Iron-Sights with MRDS

In 2011, at Norwich University, a study was done comparing the accurate use of conventional open-sights (three-dot style) against one model red-dot sight from the Trijicon corporation (an RMR model from that period).[1]

Trijicon RMR 2

Shooters used Glock 19 pistols, with the following results:

Stages of Fire		Iron-Sights Shots Fired – #Hits		Red-Dot Sight Shots Fired – #Hits
Stage 1 / 15 yards slow fire		130 / 97 75%		137 / 137 98%
Stage 2 / 5 yards rapid fire		260 / 248 95%		280 / 274 99%
Stage 3 / 10 yards rapid fire		130 / 105 81%		140 / 136 96%
Stage 4 / 10 yards rapid fire, multiple threats		132 / 110 83%		144 / 138 96%

The study's conclusion was that the red-dot optic used in this study (the Trijicon RMR) proved more effective than traditional iron-sights, even when fired by experienced firearm users. In addition, it was mentioned that the training time for those using MRDS, as opposed to the iron-sight users, was reduced.[2]

The use of the MRDS permits shooters to see their sidearm's aiming point (most generally an illuminated red-dot) on their target, which is also in focus at the very same moment. I suggest this is the critical difference between the two sighting systems, and will, at some time in the future, eliminate the use of iron-sights as the standard method of sighting used for most sidearms, excluding all but the smallest "pocket" size handguns.

*

Testing Protocol Design for MRDS

To-date I am unaware of any professionally developed testing protocol which would be suitable for determining whether or not a particular model of MRDS would be practical, or task related, in order to meet the needs for general handgun use. The technology is moving rapidly in this area, and keeping up with the newest sight options offered is quite a chore. At the time this book is being written, there are handgun MRDS for sale from approximately $20 dollars (toys really) up to about $600 dollars in cost. Which model is appropriate for general use? Well, it depends.

A thoughtful, task related protocol needs to be developed, based on demonstrable data as to <u>how</u> such sights will be used, and with what level of abuse might be expected to be heaped upon them. Most of the "tests" and "reviews" of MRDS I have seen are either "puff-pieces," or someone installing a favorite sight on a handgun, firing a few hundred rounds, and declaring "their" current chosen sight to be the best available.

In my reading of the reviews of many of the upper-end MRDS units, much weight is given to their being used by our nation's military forces. I am fully confident that those in military procurement understand the needs of their personnel, as well as the environments their equipment could be expected to function in, and determine the elements of their vetting process accordingly. The problem is, for general handgun use, what the military requires may not match what the average shooter is seeking in a MRDS.

Vortex Venom–Battery is Replaced from the Top

For example, in a number of tests I have seen done (by citizen testers), there is a drop-test of the sidearm performed every several hundred rounds fired. Such a test has little bearing on how handguns are used in the real world.

If such drop-testing had been incorporated during the previous century, when the majority of sworn law officers carried revolvers, many of them equipped with relatively delicate adjustable rear sights, then it is likely none of those sidearms, which served so well, for so long, would have passed.

A thoughtful, task related and practical set of criteria must be established for the adoption of red-dot sights for service use, as well as for those wishing to employee such sights on handguns intended for personal defense.

Whatever MRDS is being tested, two considerations ought to be kept in mind:

> Are these units *Practical* for the application the user wishes to put the sight?
> Are such sights *Task Related*, that is, most suitable to do the required "job" the user wishes?

Many of the claims made by manufacturers are, largely, unknowable. For example, battery life of some units is maintained to be 100,000 hours (there are 8,760 hours in a year). Perhaps. I'm uncertain how such a claim can be justified (let alone verified), or if any demonstrable data exists on which to base such representations. In any case, whether the battery life of a unit is "only" a few thousand hours, or ten times that number, it would be most prudent for red-dot batteries, used for service or personal defense, to be changed out yearly. This is the main reason I believe, in general, that a simple, easy to use, top-loading, battery replacement system ought to be high on the list of considerations for any MRDS purchase for use for other than a sporting application.

Choosing a MRDS

The variety of MRDS units now being manufactured range from "airsoft" grade models to serious $600 dollar, solidly made, service designed optics. The plethora of red-dot optics is confusing. Fortunately, there are a number of MRDS now available worthy of consideration for general use.

Burris Fast Fire III–Battery is Replaced from the Top

One of the distinctions of these sights is the method of replacing their batteries. Although there are fine sights out there that require the user to remove the entire sight from the handgun when changing the battery, I tend to shy away from such models. Every time you remove such a sight from its mounted position, it would only be prudent to sight-in the pistol again, to make sure the visible dot matches the pistol's point of impact. I find that a bit annoying, and, depending on circumstances, impractical.

For this reason, my preference is that all battery changes should be done with the sight remaining attached to the sidearm.

Models of MRDS Currently Available and Sight Mounting Options

One appropriate method, when affixing a MRDS to a pistol, is to procure handguns already designed for their installation.

There are a number of handgun manufacturers who now supply some of their pistol models crafted with a mounting option already in place for these optics. Such models include:

➤ Glock Modular Optic System (MOS) for their models 19, 17, 34, 35, 40 and 41
➤ S&W M&P CORE series
➤ FNH FNX 45 Tactical
➤ ATI FXH-45
➤ Sig Sauer RX series

Do keep in mind, these pistols are generally designed so that a blank section at the top of the slide is removed, and a plate with the proper configuration for screw holes for the red-dot sight being used, is put in its place.

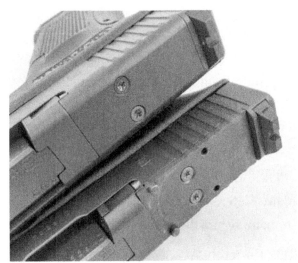

Glock MOS, With and Without Cover Plate on Pistol

There is another option. There are companies which offer the milling of slides designed for specific red-dot models. Such an option, if chosen, makes for a nice, secure, low mounting of the sight. Prices vary among those offering this service. Keep in mind, once done, only that model sight may now be used on that firearm's slide.

Another option uses a system in which the rear sight is removed from the pistol, a "blank" inserted in its place (the now empty dovetail for the rear sight), and a mounting plate is then screwed into the threaded holes in the blank, with the MRDS then attached to the plate. I have photos of such an installation for readers to review. For informal shooting purposes this is an inexpensive, and simple way, to mount a red-dot sight.

Glock 17 with Vortex Venom on a Plate Mount

Ruger LC9 with Galloway Precision Mount and Red-Dot Sight

Two Variations for MRDS Mounting using Rearsight Dovetails

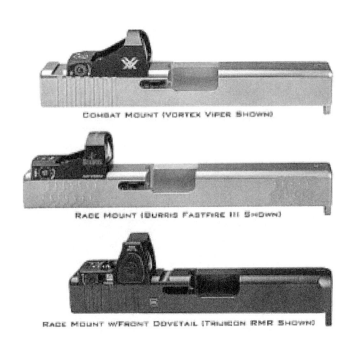

COMBAT MOUNT (VORTEX VIPER SHOWN)

RACE MOUNT (BURRIS FASTFIRE III SHOWN)

RACE MOUNT w/FRONT DOVETAIL (TRIJICON RMR SHOWN)

Lone Wolf "Slide Melt" Options for Glock Model Pistols

Some Current Models of Red-Dot Sights Suitable for Service Use

Just a few of the currently available optical sight models suitable for such use are mentioned here. These models would serve well for "serious" duty or personal defense purposes:

Trijicon RMR

The Trijicon RMR models of sight are strongly built, excellent units. Indeed, for many in the field they are considered the "gold standard" of MRDS. The Trijicon sights are robust and battle proven, having seen much service over the previous twenty years by our military forces. These sights are expensive. However, I do see two significant issues in regard their general use, particularly in law enforcement:

> ➢ Battery replacement requires the sight to be removed from its mount, and it is possible the firearm would need to be re-zeroed when this is done. In addition,
> ➢ The highly protective "horns" of the RMS sight cover a goodly amount of a shooter's view when aiming at the target.

Leupold Delta Point

For general as well as law enforcement use the Leupold Delta Point models are excellent sights. These sights are:

> ➢ Strongly built,
> ➢ The sight is always "on" but goes "to sleep" after a short period of non-use,
> ➢ The battery is easily replaced from the top of the sight (the sight remains in place on the firearm),
> ➢ The "window" is relatively large, the glass inside is clear, and,
> ➢ A co-witnessing, adjustable, rear sight may be easily installed on these units.*

*Co-witness sights; Iron-sights that may be seen through the lens of the MRDS. Effectively creating a back-up sighting system.

The battery life of such units would be approximately six months. A battery of the type used in this sight is about as costly as a single round of service type ammunition.

Shield RMS

This is a well-made sight which offers a number of advantages:

- ➢ The design is compact,
- ➢ Battery changes easily from a side drawer,
- ➢ The sight is always "on,"
- ➢ Battery life is said to be long,
- ➢ It's very light in weight (0.61 ounces),
- ➢ The sight has a built-in rear-sight, for co-witnessing with the pistol's front sight

Shield RMS Showing Open Battery Compartment

MRDS for Sporting and Recreational Shooting

Vortex Venom

The author has two (2) such units, one for a Glock 17, 9mm handgun, the other for a Ruger MK IV, 22/45, .22 caliber pistol. Both sights use three (3) MOA size dots, and have performed admirably. This model has a wide "window" and the points of impact on these pistols have not moved after many thousands of rounds after having been fired. The other advantages of this sight are:

> The batteries are replaced from the top,
> Warranty is reported to be excellent, and,
> Cost of this sight is reasonable.

Burris Fast Fire III

As with the Vortex Venom, I have two of these sights. Both use the six (6) MOA size dot. One is attached to a Glock 17, 9mm, the other to a Ruger LC9 Pro 9mm. What I've noted above about the Vortex Venom is equally true for the Burris model:

> The battery is replaced from the top,
> Warranty is reported to be excellent, and,
> Cost of the unit is at the mid-point of useable red-dot sights.

Co-Witness of Sights

If so desired, there are a number of ways the users of MRDS may also utilize their handgun's iron-sights as a "back-up" option. The most common method is for the installation of "suppressor" sights. As these sights are substantially higher than conventional sights, they may (in most cases) be viewed through the window of the red-dot sights, thus eliminating the concern for mechanical, electrical or battery failures.

The author has not had an opportunity to conduct an experiment with MRDS which I believe would address this issue in an easy to use and intuitive way. As the window housing of red-dot sights form, for lack of a better term, a large "peep-sight" (aperture sight), then I suggest this large round part of the red-dot sight (in the same manner as when using a "Ghost-Ring" sight), might well be used for aiming a pistol at close range when the tall front sight is placed in the middle of this ring (the window opening of the red-dot sight).

Such use of the rear window opening of MRDS, if testing proves this to be practical, might eliminate the need for a rear back-up open sight, at least at very close range.

Delta Point Pro with Accessory Rear Sight Attached.
Top Battery Compartment is Visible.

Small Battery Tester

I suggest it would be prudent, when out in the field with a handgun utilizing a MRDS, to have at least one spare battery for that model sight with you.

I would also urge you to purchase an inexpensive battery tester, and ensure that both the battery in your sight, as well as any spares you have with you, possess sufficient battery life to be useful.

High quality, name brand batteries should be purchased for use in your sights, unless such sights are used simply for general plinking and sport shooting only.

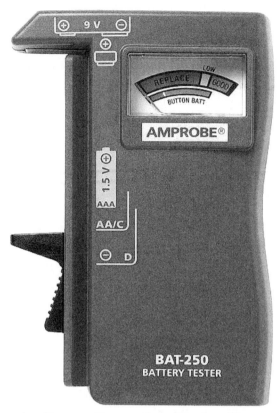

An Inexpensive Battery Tester, Suitable for "Button" Batteries

Conclusion

The technology involved in the manufacture of MRDS will continue to evolve and improve. I believe, as their popularity increases, the cost for such sights will go down, their designs will become ever more practical, they will be made more robust, and battery life will be enhanced.

The ability for shooters to clearly see both their target, as well as their aiming point, on a single plane of focus, should increase the individual's ability to both identify as well as hit their targets. Training times should be reduced, and, from my personal experience, sport shooters will derive additional enjoyment when firing their handguns.

Partial List of MRDS Manufacturers (Alphabetically)

Burris
https://www.burrisoptics.com/sights/fastfire-red-dot-sights

C-More STS2
https://cmore.com/Category/reddot

Doctor Sight
http://docterusa.com/docter-red-dot-sights/

Eotech MRDS
http://www.eotechinc.com/holographic-weapon-sights/mini-red-dot-sight-mrds

JP Jpoint
https://www.jprifles.com/1.6.1.php

Leupold
https://www.leupold.com/product-series/deltapoint-reflex-sight

Meopta (MeoRed/Meosight III)
https://www.meoptasportsoptics.com/us/produkt/red-dot-sights-meosight-iii-3412/

Shield Sights
https://www.shieldpsd.com/portfolio-posts/reflex-mini-sight

Sightmark
http://sightmark.com/category.php?cat=56

Trijicon
https://www.trijicon.com/na_en/products/product1.php?id=RMR

Vortex
http://www.vortexoptics.com/category/red_dots

Richard P. Rosenthal

Suppressors References

[1] *Comparative Pistol Project Final Report*, Department of Justice Studies and Sociology, Norwich University, James e. Ryan, Robin Adler, February 24, 2011
http://soldiersystems.net/blog1/wp-content/uploads/2014/03/2011_Norwich_Study_RMRvIronSights.pdf

[2] ibid.

Manual of Arms

(Plus A Few Miscellaneous Matters)

By necessity, some of the material covered next would also fit neatly into the chapter on Firearms Safety. None the less, as the only rational way a person should be trained to handle firearms is to do so safely, there is little to be lost by this material's inclusion at this point in the book. I will do my best to avoid redundancy.

I use the term "Manual of Arms" as a convenience. Perhaps the more correct, and original, meaning of the words is most often that of a manual used to describe the proper manner, by the numbers, on how to load and fire the very complex flintlock rifles of several hundred years ago. Included was how to drill with these arms. My meaning is the outlining of the correct and best way to safely handle a handgun, including proper loading, and unloading techniques, as well as a number of other necessary ancillary acts routinely performed with the sidearm.

*

Manual of Arms

Revolver

> ➢ Present revolver. How to hand a revolver to another safely.
> ➢ How to carry a revolver safely when out of its holster.
> ➢ Loading and unloading techniques.

Ruger MKII Heavy Barrel Target Pistol ~ .22 Caliber

Richard P. Rosenthal

Present Revolver Safely to Another:

From time to time it may be appropriate and necessary for you to hand a revolver over to another person. Your goal is to do so safely, and in a professional manner.

At no time is the shooter's finger on the revolver's trigger during this act!

> ➤ Hold the revolver by the grip, with the muzzle pointed to the ground.

With the muzzle still pointed down;

> ➤ Push, pull or press in on the cylinder release latch, as appropriate for your model of handgun, and,
> ➤ Grasping the barrel, push the cylinder open with your index finger. Then,
> ➤ Hand the revolver to the person receiving it, butt first.

This is a safe and secure method permitting the transfer of possession of a revolver from one person to another, whether loaded or unloaded. If you are left handed the procedure is the same. Simply place the handgun in the right hand prior to finally executing this maneuver.

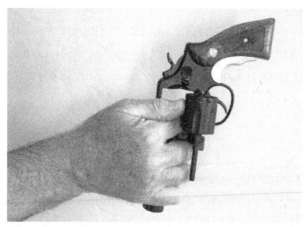

Handing a Revolver to Another Person Safely

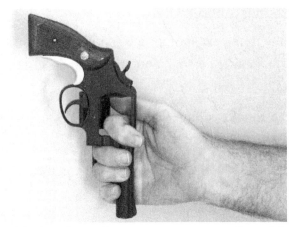

You may safely hand another person your revolver this way, with or without live rounds in the chamber.

*

Safely Walking About with a Revolver:

The best way to carry and walk about with a handgun out of its holster is with the cylinder open and the shooter's fingers holding the handgun around the top strap. I find that even though the handgun is perfectly safe at this point, it is prudent to have the revolver's muzzle pointed down to the ground as well (butt of the handgun pointed in the direction of travel).

Obviously, single-action revolvers cannot have their cylinders readily left open. In this case, place the handgun's hammer at half-cock and open the loading gate, or, if a Ruger of modern design, simply open the loading gate. In either case, keep the muzzle pointed to the ground.

The trigger finger will <u>always</u> remain outside of the trigger guard during this procedure.

*

There are a number of techniques recommended for the unloading and reloading of revolvers, with advantages and disadvantages for each. Which one/s you will wish to master will depend on the application you are going to put the handgun to. For example, are you carrying a small or large frame revolver? If so, how do you carry your spare ammunition? Speedloaders (rather bulky for a concealment handgun), speed-strips (somewhat slow to get into action but great to throw in a pocket as back-up ammo), half or full-moon clips (stamped pieces of metal capable of holding rounds of ammunition), or an ammo pouch. If a pouch, is it a 3X3, 2X2X2 or one that simply holds five or six spare rounds within a single compartment, all of which dump out at once?

Whatever technique you use, it should be practiced with some regularity in order to master the needed movements for a successful reload to become second nature.

The method for combat loading a revolver described next is most suitable for short barrel, smaller frame handguns. I also use it when reloading my K-frame S&W police service revolver, but that's because it was the technique taught to me at the NYPD, and one I've taught many other shooters over the years. Its advantages are, it gives the shooter the most control of the unloading and loading process, particularly with a short barrel pocket revolver, while using individual rounds of ammunition instead of when utilizing a mechanical (speedloader) reloading device. It's also useful technique when executing a partial reload.

In its defense I think it only fair to point out that this technique is the one used by Jerry Miculek when he set the world record of twelve shots in under three seconds in 1999!

S&W Model 19, with 4" Barrel and Round Butt ~ .357 Magnum

Combat loading the revolver:

> ➢ Operate the cylinder release latch with your right hand thumb.
> ➢ With the left hand; use the middle and ring finger and push out on the cylinder. The index finger goes alongside the barrel.
> ➢ Pointing your muzzle up, and while keeping the two fingers pushing out on the cylinder, place your pinky under the hammer spur and the pad of your thumb on the tip of the ejector rod.
> ➢ Push down briskly on the rod (Only One Time! DO NOT PUMP THE ROD!!) and let your thumb slip off the rod to the left (caution: just to the side is located the sharp edge of the revolver's crane).
> ➢ Permit the empty cases to fall free of the mechanism (gravity is your friend).

–Keep the muzzle up and/or at an angle away from the open cylinder or malfunctions will occur–

Now, while bending your wrist, twist the revolver so the muzzle is pointing in the direction of the ground (gravity remains your friend).

Do not materially change the position of the fingers.

> ➢ Reload the handgun either with individual rounds or the speedloading device of your choice.
> ➢ Engage your target, or holster your sidearm, as appropriate.

*

Semi-Auto Pistols

The manual of arms with a semi-auto pistol will, of course, differ from that of the revolver. A word of caution, handling the semi-auto requires more deliberate thinking on the part of the user than does the revolver. Don't misunderstand my last comment. You had certainly best know what you're doing with a revolver before picking it up, as well as be familiar with the firearm's mechanism. It's just that the semi-auto is somewhat less forgiving of errors and omissions.

A revolver, by a glance at even a closed cylinder, will indicate by the round's visible rims to the user that the chambers are loaded. Not so the semi-auto. Once the slide is closed and in battery, except (and only in some models) for a small rise in either the extractor or some other subtle mechanical indicator that there is a round in the chamber, any cartridge contained therein would not be readily visible to the shooter.

In the chapter on safety I will go into far more detail as to how one should safely handle a semi-auto pistol. At this point in the discussion I simply wish the reader to be cognizant of the inherent danger of holding a pistol in your hand while at the same time you are uncertain (or worse, certain!) that it is either loaded, or unloaded. Treat all guns as if they had a round in the chamber and were ready to fire. Please.

*

The following material does firmly overlap into my discussion on firearms safety. So be it.

<u>Present a Semi-Auto Pistol Safely to Another:</u>

Two very important things must be understood and complied with when preparing to hand a semi-auto handgun to another;

1-Your finger has no business being anywhere near the firearm's trigger!!

2-You must, must, must –did I mention you must? – <u>first remove the pistol's magazine prior to manipulating the firearm's action</u> when engaged in an effort to make it safe. Failing to do so is very likely the greatest single cause of negligent discharges with semi-automatic pistols that I can think of. By ignoring this caution, you *will* inadvertently chamber a round in your pistol while in the act of –at least in your mind– making it safe. A frightfully dangerous situation to be in. And a lethal one. You have been warned.

With your finger off the trigger and the weapon's magazine removed;

> With the muzzle pointed in a safe direction, pull the slide to the rear and, if possible, lock it in place.
> In either hand, grasp the pistol by its slide so that the muzzle is pointed to the ground, butt pointed forward.

Before working the action of any firearm, you MUST –repeat– MUST remove the source of ammunition FIRST!!

You may now hand the pistol to another or safely walk about with the gun in your hand. An alternate way to properly walk around with an unloaded semi-auto pistol is, with the slide locked to the rear, hold the firearm by the butt as you would prior to shooting the handgun, finger off and away from the trigger, with the muzzle pointed straight up in the air.

It might be fair to add that while the instructions I've presented above are correct and useful, the safest way to walk about with a handgun, loaded or not, is with the gun in a secure holster attached to your body.

Understand that the goal, when walking around with an unloaded handgun while among other people, is to put those around you at ease. The various techniques I've discussed here will serve two purposes for you; you will be viewed as a knowledgeable and experienced handler of firearms, and, all those near you will be safe from the consequences of an accidental discharge.

*

Internal Safeties of Modern Handguns

I am frequently asked whether it is safe to carry a round either in the chamber of a modern semi-auto pistol, or with a round directly under the hammer of a modern double-action revolver. The quick and dirty answer is, "yes." Now, for a bit of detailed discussion on the matter.

First the disclaimer. This issue is limited to semi-auto pistols that are designed to be; a striker-fired "safety action," are double-action only, or have some sort of hammer-drop mechanism incorporated in their design. As in regard revolvers, again I am only talking about modern designs which either have a transfer bar incorporated in their design or possess some other internal safety (S&W type) that precludes firing the handgun unless the trigger is held fully to the rear.

With the modern S&W handgun there are a number of variants. In all cases, unless the revolver's trigger is physically held to the rear as the hammer falls, such a handgun in sound mechanical condition will not discharge. During safety classes of mine I demonstrate this fact by taking my venerable S&W model 10 service handgun, unloaded of course, and, after cocking the revolver's hammer fully to the rear, I insert the eraser end of a pencil down its muzzle.

First, with the muzzle pointing up, I simply pull the trigger. The pencil is generally jettisoned out from the gun's muzzle, the impact of the firing pin having sufficient force to cause the pencil to be ejected from the barrel. I next re-cock the gun, insert the pencil and, this time using a metal pointer, tap the revolver's trigger. This causes the hammer to fall forward. The pencil, however, does not move, as the firing pin could not make contact with it due to the fact that the trigger had come forward before the gun's hammer could. This demonstrates to my students the proper functioning of the firearm's internal safety.

A revolver with a transfer bar system is, if anything, an even safer sidearm. This type of mechanism, designed over a century ago by the Iver Johnson firearms company, and referred to by them as the "Hammer the Hammer" system, is wonderfully simple in design and execution. The revolver's hammer never comes in contact with the gun's firing pin. In order to discharge the handgun a metal bar must first come up and interface with the firing pin and face of the hammer, which can only take place when the gun's trigger is held to the rear.

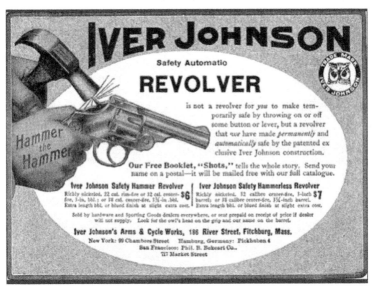

Iver Johnson "Safety Automatic" Revolver Ad

In the advertising of the period they (the Iver Johnson Company) routinely show a depiction of one of their revolver's hammers being struck by a hammer, thus the advertising slogan.

There are several variants of recently manufactured semi-auto pistol which are intended to be carried with a round in their chambers, albeit too many, and too varied in type, for me to discuss in their entirety here. A few that are commonly seen are;

Glocks, Sig Sauer (many of their models but not all), S&W pistols, Heckler and Koch designs, specific Walthers, Rugers, Berettas and many others.

The simplest way to determine if a pistol with exposed hammer would be safe to carry with a round in the chamber would be the answer to the question; can the hammer be lowered without the shooter touching the gun's trigger? If the answer is "no," then my advice to the average shooter would be to avoid using that handgun for service or self-defense purposes.

Here we come to the proverbial "elephant in the room." The Colt 1911 series of pistol. This pattern of handgun (and there are many variations, by many manufacturers, in all sizes and calibers), evolved from a 1900 Browning design, and, although over a century old, remains very popular with shooters, as well as with some members of the military and law enforcement. For the model's adherents, a common method of carry with this handgun is with the gun in "condition one," or cocked and locked. That means, the firearm has a round in its chamber, the gun's hammer is fully to the rear, and its manual thumb safety is "on," or "on safe."

For many users of this sidearm, particularly those who have received extensive –and recurrent– training with this model, they manage to get along just fine carrying their pistols in this manner. On occasion, especially with folks who think that by the mere act of purchasing an expensive piece of equipment, firing a box or two of ammo down range, and chatting about their prowess with their buddies, they are sufficiently competent, have had enough training, and developed adequate muscle memory in order to properly operate this fairly complex mechanism, things don't always work out so well.

If you are truly interested in investing the time, effort and money in learning how to properly, competently and safely operate a 1911 Colt, or one of its many variants, then please go about it. If your goal is to have, for service and personal protection use, a practical sidearm that may not be quite so demanding of your time and efforts, you might well consider a handgun of more recent design.

I don't wish to appear to be picking on the 1911 pattern pistol. There are a number of other interesting, indeed, beautifully crafted pistols, that I would consider only for recreational shooting and collection purposes. Models such as the Sig Sauer P210, Broomhandle Mauser of 1896, the P-08 (Luger), any of the Colt pocket pistols of the early twentieth century, just to name a few, are all truly fine handguns, well-crafted and worthy of ownership. Just don't attempt to carry one with a round in the chamber.

I hope I'm being clear here. The reason I'm not recommending the 1911 type pistol, or other handguns of older design is, simply, that there is a far greater likelihood of an accidental discharge when a person either attempts to lower the hammer on a live round, or when the user depends on a mechanical safety to keep a fully spring-loaded firing pin in its place with a loaded pistol. Newer designs are, quite simply, safer to carry loaded.

Glock handguns, as well as several other model pistols, can never have their "hammers" lowered, as they have none, just a spring powered striker (or firing pin). They are safe to carry with a round in the chamber. Just keep your finger (or any other object) away from the trigger unless you intend to discharge the piece.

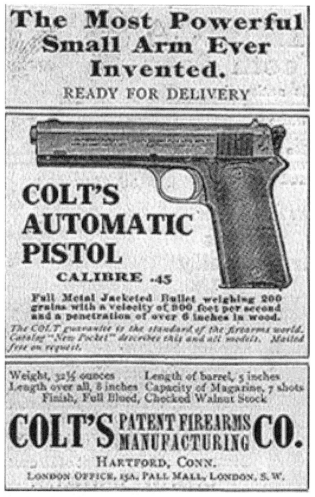

The Most Powerful
Small Arm Ever
Invented.

READY FOR DELIVERY

COLT'S AUTOMATIC PISTOL

CALIBRE .45

Full Metal Jacketed Bullet weighing 200 grains with a velocity of 900 feet per second and a penetration of over 6 inches in wood.

The COLT guarantee is the standard of the firearms world. Catalog "New Pocket" describes this and all models. Mailed free on request.

Weight, 32½ ounces   Length of barrel, 5 inches
Length over all, 8 inches   Capacity of Magazine, 7 shots
Finish, Full Blued, Checked Walnut Stock

COLT'S PATENT FIREARMS MANUFACTURING CO.

HARTFORD, CONN.
LONDON OFFICE, 15A, PALL MALL, LONDON, S. W.

An Early Model Colt .45. Note the Lack of any Safety.
This handgun was Never Intended by Browning to be Carried
"Cocked and Locked."

How to safely lower the hammer, on a chambered round, for other model semi-auto pistol suitable for carry for service or self-defense purposes would depend on the model under discussion. On Sig models some have a hammer-lowering mechanism. These handguns, which fire their first round in double-action mode then revert to single-action, have a lever on the left side of the frame which, when pushed down, causes the hammer to come forward (safely), putting the handgun back into a double-action condition. Other model pistols use an assortment of mechanical hammer-lowering mechanisms. When you acquire a new pistol, you are obligated to learn, understand, and master, the mechanism. Furthermore, your finger has no business being near the trigger when engaged in lowering the hammer of any pistol of modern design.

*

Speedloader being used with S&W 10

A note on speedloaders. A number of very effective devices have been developed for the rapid reloading of revolvers. They are manufactured by a number of reputable companies. These include HKS, Safariland, as well as others. Each design has its followers. When carrying a service-size revolver the use of speedloaders permits the quick reloading of the handgun. If their bulk does not conflict with the purpose you are carrying the sidearm, I'd suggest you invest in a few for use in your revolver.

Another method of ammunition carry is the Bianchi or TUFF Speed Strip. Although slower than a speedloader, these neoprene strips, each holding (generally) from five to six rounds of the caliber of your choice, are a good way to carry spare rounds in a jacket pocket. I own around a dozen of these loaders and salt them away in my various coat pockets. You never know when your revolver is going to need a reload.

Moon and half-moon clips are an old idea that seems to have become quite popular again. These clips (yes, "clips" is the proper term) were designed around the First World War. Revolvers were being manufactured for the war effort in .45 ACP caliber. As this cartridge has no rim, once fired a pencil or stick was needed to empty the spent shells from their chambers.

These half-moon clips were developed to solve this problem. The rimless shells were inserted into the clip openings (three rounds per clip). Then the three shells, as a unit, could be both inserted into, and ejected, as one, from the revolver.

The modern variation is a full-moon, or simply, a "moon-clip." Six rounds are held captured by this thin sheet of metal and inserted and ejected as one. This makes for a rapid reload/unload sequence but precludes the possibility of a partial reload during a lull in the action. None the less, I suspect the tactical advantages they offer far outweigh whatever downsides they may possess.

Whatever type of speedloader you opt to purchase, do two things for your sake. First, ensure the speedloader operates with your handgun without interference from some part of the revolver, most often the left side grip panel. Second, practice using the device. The time to figure out if you have the operation down pat is at the firing range, not a micro second after your handgun just went dry in a gun fight.

My old Colt Detective Special .38 Special caliber revolver.

This Colt Detective Special served me well while I was a detective in the NYPD. It was mostly carried as a "back-up" handgun, to be used after my S&W model 10 service revolver went "dry." Keep in mind, a modern police officer, armed with a Glock 17, carries eighteen rounds of ammunition in their sidearm. That's the amount of ammunition I had on me, combined, with two, six shot revolvers, plus a six round ammunition pouch. And, yes, when on duty as a detective I carried my S&W service handgun as well as the more compact Colt.

But that's not my point here. Note the ground down escutcheon on the grip panel of the revolver. That was needed to permit me to use speedloaders with this handgun.

Firearms Safety!

Guns are Always Loaded!

"Those people who are routinely around firearms either have had, or will have, an unintentional discharge."

Lt. Frank MaGee, former CO, NYPD Firearms & Tactics Section

*

Safety with Firearms

Firearm safety is not solely about safety. It is also important to understand that how those around you observe your handling of firearms will immediately reveal to them how much you know about firearms. Their opinion of you will be formed by your actions. If you wave the muzzle around, put your finger on the gun's trigger to no purpose, don't routinely check to see if a firearm handed to you, or one which is newly picked up by you, is loaded, you'll be branded as a nimrod.

I'd like to begin with the four fundamentals of safety. These are not mere platitudes, offered with a wink and nod. These rules are important, and must be memorized, understood and obeyed;

Four Fundamentals of Safety:

- ➤ Treat every firearm as if it is loaded
- ➤ Always point the muzzle in a safe direction
- ➤ Be certain of your target and what lays beyond
- ➤ Keep your finger outside of –and off– the trigger until ready to shoot

Treat Every Firearm as If It Is Loaded

Why is it that so many "unloaded" firearms accidentally discharge and kill people? Simply stated, because they weren't unloaded correctly in the first place! In a moment we'll go into detail about the unloading of specific types of firearms, but I'd like to begin with a story.

This happened many years ago, to two police officers working for a New York City police agency (there are quite a few in the city) which was <u>not</u> the NYPD. The two officers, along with their girlfriends, had gone upstate New York on a "hunting" trip. Inside their cabin the couples began to playfully horse-around. One of the guy's, along with the other man's female companion, went into a bedroom and, kidding around, tossed out articles of clothing through the open door, in a manner to suggest, jokingly, that they were undressing.

The other officer, also in a playful mood, took hold of his five shot "off-duty" revolver, unloaded it (or at least he thought that he had), and, when the young woman came out of the room, pointed the gun at her, made some comment about this is what she gets for fooling around on him, and pulled the trigger. The gun discharged, killing her.

A horrible tragedy? Certainly. Preventable? That is equally certain.

The officer violated three of the four safety rules, not to mention the fact that he improperly unloaded his revolver (a subject we'll take up in greater detail in a moment). He treated the gun as if it were unloaded. He pointed the gun at a person he had no intention of harming. Lastly, he pulled the trigger on his handgun while having no intention of actually firing the weapon.

*

Unloading Revolvers:

Every time you unload a revolver you must perform the following actions:

- ➢ While the muzzle is pointed in the safest possible direction,
- ➢ Open the cylinder, then,
- ➢ Perform a proper unload procedure.
- ➢ Look (really look) at the chambers of the revolver's cylinder to ensure that they are empty.

> ➤ Count (yes, count – as I do every time!) the number of rounds you have in the palm of your hand.

*

<u>Unloading Semi-Auto Pistols:</u>

Every time you unload a semi-auto pistol you must perform the following actions:

> ➤ With the muzzle pointed in the safest possible direction,
> ➤ Remove the magazine.

You must ***ALWAYS*** remove the firearm's source of ammunition (in this case, the pistol's magazine) before attempting to remove a round from the chamber!

> ➤ Pull the gun's slide to the rear and, if possible, lock it in place, then,
> ➤ look (really look) at the chamber of the pistol, to ensure that it is empty. Then, stick your finger in the chamber as well.

What is a safe direction? That depends. If you're at the range, then the answer is simple. Point the muzzle downrange. On the third floor of a four-floor walkup? I'm not sure there is a safe direction for the absolutely safe unloading of a handgun at such a location.

I know a retired federal agent, when once assigned to a crowded office, who created an unloading box from an old, out of service bullet resistant vest, which he stored in a no-longer useful briefcase. Great idea. The NYPD (and the Wellfleet PD after I got there) had Safety Stations for loading and unloading firearms. These were tubes of heavy metal, painted a gaudy orange, half filled with sand. The officers firearms muzzles were to go into the open ports cut into the side of these stations when loading and unloading their weapons. Although it never happened when I was around (or ever, in the case of Wellfleet) my rule was a simple one. If a firearm discharged while the officer's muzzle was in that Safety Station's port, neither a report, nor any other action, need be taken by the officer. Should there have been an accidental discharge someplace else, well, that would have been another matter.

*

Once the cylinder of the revolver has been opened –and the method of operation of the cylinder release latch will vary with make and model of handgun– place the handgun in the left hand, second (ring) and middle fingers inside the weapon's frame wrapped around the cylinder, while pushing the cylinder fully open. This is important as you'll see in a moment.

The index (pointer or forefinger) finger rests on the outside of the barrel and the pinky goes behind the hammer, or, at least, situated at the rearmost part of the sidearm. With the sidearm's muzzle tilted slightly away from the open cylinder, the thumb is placed on the end of the ejector rod and, while your right hand is cupped under the revolver. Press down **ONE TIME** on the ejector rod, permitting the rod to run home, free of further contact with the thumb.

<u>Do Not Pump the Ejector Rod!</u> The reasons are simple; it's a completely pointless waste of time (the rod cannot go any farther out after you've done it once), and, worst of all, can sometimes lead to an empty shell case getting stuck between the "star" and the frame (the star has various names, depending on the manufacturers nomenclature, including "ejector" and "extractor." I find the term "star" most descriptive of this part's shape. It's that part of the mechanism that is pushed out from the rear of the cylinder bringing with it any loaded rounds or empty shell casings).

Now, I realize the next part is going to sound patronizing. That's not my intent and the advice is important to remember. You are to look, really <u>look,</u> at the empty chambers in front of you. You must then count each and every round you are holding in your hand. I ask you to believe me when I tell you that when I unload any of my revolvers, this is the exact procedure I go through. Every time. If you follow suit it will preclude the possibility of a tragedy occurring to you with an "unloaded" revolver.

Back to the matter of how people wind up injuring, sometime killing, others, after they've "unloaded" their revolvers? It's because when the cylinder was opened the user didn't perform two critical actions;

1-The cylinder was only partially opened (most often with a little flopping motion so often seen in movies and on the TV) and the rounds permitted to fall out by their own accord, then,

2-They didn't count the number of rounds which fell out of the cylinder into their open hand.

This type of improper unloading technique ensures that, from time to time, a single round will remain in one of the revolver's cylinder chambers, due to the fact that the cylinder was not opened completely, blocking the round's exit, as well as the ejector rod not having been used in the process. Should the handgun be from the S&W line, when the cylinder is then closed the next chamber coming up for firing will contain that hidden round.

Quite a few years ago, when a NYPD homicide detective, there was an incident in our squad room. I wasn't there, but was told by someone who was that a few of the detectives had engaged in a debate as to which direction their revolvers cylinders rotated (Colts would generally rotate to the right, S&W to the left). Now, had I been there I would have pointed out that if they just looked at the cuts around the circumference of the cylinder, the ones designed for catching the cylinder stop, they would have noticed the cuts were –more or less– shaped like little arrows. The direction of the "arrow" is the same direction in which a revolver's cylinder rotates!

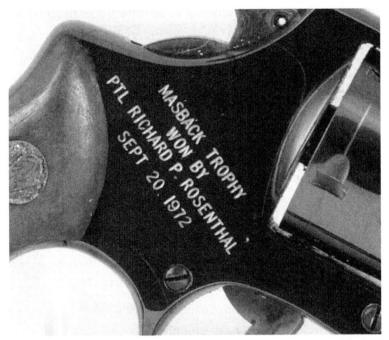

The "Arrows" in the Cylinder Point in the Direction of Rotation!

Alas, I was not there. The guys decided to determine in which direction their revolvers cylinders rotated by empirical observation. So, a senior detective, sitting at a desk at the rear of the office, "unloaded" his handgun and, a moment later while conducting his little test, experienced what we might call an "unfortunate incident."

According to my source, a micro-second after the loud bang of the discharging handgun not a soul was to be seen in the squad room! Remarkable!

<u>Always point the muzzle in a safe direction</u>

–&–

<u>Be certain of your target and what lies beyond</u>

Think of your firearm's muzzle as having a laser beam coming out of it (Rockland County New York Police Academy chief firearms instructor

74

Peter Tarley taught me that analogy). Anywhere that laser crosses has the potential to destroy things. Respect where you, and others, point that muzzle. Don't tolerate people who are careless with how, and in what direction, they point the muzzle of their firearms.

Furthermore, bullets travel significant distances after they have been fired. The maximum lethal range of small arms firearms projectiles, when fired on the earth's surface, with its gravity and atmosphere, comes about at an approximate barrel angle of around 35 degrees (I use the word "approximate" as there are too many variables for the purposes of our discussion here for me to go into greater technical detail in regard the matter). If on the moon (no air – in a vacuum) the angle of maximum range would be attained at a barrel angle of 45 degrees.

*

Approximate maximum ranges of:

.22 long rifle	±1 mile
30'06	±3 miles
50 BMG	5 miles

Handgun rounds generally have a nominal danger range of a little over one mile.

There have been a number of incidents that highlight the caution that should be taken when discharging a firearm. One such incident took place in Brooklyn, New York, in July 1967. An NYPD detective lieutenant was driving along the Belt Parkway (this roadway runs along the edge of Brooklyn, the Atlantic Ocean bordering one side). The day was clear and warm. Driving directly ahead of him he noticed an attractive young woman (she was seventeen years old) at the wheel of a sports sedan.

It struck the lieutenant strange when the car began to slowly move from one lane, over to the next, then the next, all without signaling. It became alarming when the car ran up onto the road's grassy side and crashed into some bushes and a tree. The lieutenant immediately pulled over to assist the injured driver.

What he found at the wheel of the accident vehicle was a dying young woman who, as it soon became apparent, had suffered a single gunshot wound to the head, the bullet entering from the open rear window of her small auto.

What had transpired was, a man, out on his fishing boat about a mile from the incident, decided to fire a few rounds from his .303 British Enfield rifle. One of the projectiles, after striking the water, traveled the nearly mile distance to the victim's head, killing her almost instantly.[1]

I read about a similar incident in New Jersey. This took place, if I recall correctly, on a July 4th day during the 1970s. Some young men were shooting at turtles by a pond. One of the rounds either struck the water and bounced, or one of the young men had raised his sights a bit, I don't recall the exact set of facts. A few moments later, about three miles away, a woman heard a thump outside her home. She knew her husband was on the roof, doing some repair work. Stepping outside she found her husband, lying dead on the ground. A single gunshot wound to his lower back had killed him, the round coming from the young men firing their rifle so many miles away.

Some much more recent accidents highlight the danger:

Atlanta GA, January 5, 2010–A four-year-old boy was killed by a falling bullet fired two miles away from where he was attending a church service.

Marquel Peters was seated with his parents (*in a church*) when the bullet, fired outside as part of New Year celebrations, came through the church roof and struck him on the head.

The toddler collapsed at the feet of his parents who had no idea what had caused the gaping wound in his head.

It was only as doctors tried to save his life that they realized what had happened. Ballistic experts believe the ammunition came from an AK 47 assault rifle fired more than two miles away from where the child was attending a service at the Church of God of Prophecy in Atlanta, Georgia. [2]

*

FREDERICKSBURG, Ohio (AP) December 20, 2011-- A man cleaning his muzzle-loading rifle shot the gun into the air, accidentally killing a 15-year-old Amish girl driving a horse-drawn buggy more than a mile away, a sheriff said Tuesday.

Rachel Yoder was shot in the head Thursday night while traveling to her home in Wayne County, between Columbus and Akron. She had attended a Christmas party for employees, most of them under 18 years old, at an Amish produce farm and was riding home alone when she was shot, Wayne County sheriff's Capt. Douglas Hunter said.

The man had fired the gun in the air about 1.5 miles from where Yoder was shot, Zimmerly said. State investigators were checking the rifle for a ballistics match, he said.[3]

*

It is your responsibility to know where the muzzle of your firearm is pointing as well as where a round will travel before pulling the trigger.

*

Keep your finger outside the trigger guard and off the trigger until ready to shoot

"On Target ~ Finger On Trigger"

"Off Target ~ Finger Off Trigger"

People ignoring this rule are a major reason for so many accidental and negligent firearms discharges. The trigger, with few exceptions (take-down, maintenance, etc.), is to be used only to discharge the handgun.

Therefore, the shooter's trigger finger, until just prior to firing the gun, should be kept out of, and alongside, the trigger guard.

Since virtually all shooting commences either from the holster or with the handgun at the ready position, no time whatever is lost by the shooter keeping the trigger finger off of, and away from, the trigger until just prior to firing.

People get in trouble with firearms not only by putting their finger on their firearms trigger. Sometimes other objects take the place of a person's digits, with unfortunate consequences.

Some years ago, while in the NYPD, I worked with a very nice guy, a detective, Nick.

Nick, as did all detectives, qualified at that time, yearly, with the Stevens model 311 double-barrel shotgun. I realize most readers will pooh-pooh the idea that an "ancient" double-barrel 12 gauge was standard police issue in the NYPDD, finding such a firearm to be "quaint." Thing is, they'd be dead wrong. The gun was stone reliable, very simple to operate (making it easy to train a person to use –thus a practical issue weapon), and, with a double load of magnum 00 buckshot, could put 24 pellets downrange with two pulls of the trigger. You could do a lot worse in a pinch. At combat distances, it was a very potent firearm.

When officers came to the department's Outdoor Range at Rodman's Neck (located in the north Bronx) for their annual double-barrel qualification, the firearms instructors would take the opportunity to function check whatever sidearm the detectives were carrying. Nick was wearing a blue steel S&W model 36, a plain-vanilla five shot .38 Special revolver, standard NYPD issue at the time.

Envision the scene. Those present for qualification all entered an enclosed "mess-hall" that was used, during the morning, for the checking of their sidearms. Lines could be rather long. Once an officer came up to a table, he'd present his revolver to the instructor, who would empty the handgun, run a function check, then hand the gun back to the officer, cylinder open but with the rounds put back in their chambers.

Nick, balancing his Stevens model 311 on his left hip, took his sidearm back, closed the cylinder and attempted to shove it back into his rather old –very worn and frayed– holster. This particular design used a steel spring, sandwiched between two pieces of leather, to aid in retaining the sidearm. For many years this was a popular holster design.

Well, Nick pushed, but the darn gun just wouldn't go into place. So, he pushed some more, this time really hard. Then he heard what he thought was a firecracker some wise guy had just set off nearby.

The firearms instructor in front of him said, "Son, you just shot yourself. Lie down," and took the shotgun from Nick's hands. Which was exactly what had taken place.

What had happened was, that old, long overdue for retirement holster Nick had on had been put together using cotton thread (now virtually all holsters are manufactured using Nylon thread), as was the custom of the time. The thread had begun to unravel, permitting the metal spring, which had been sandwiched between the two layers of leather, to stick out. Nick's trigger had caught on the protruding piece of metal, and, when Nick pushed down hard enough, he managed to shoot himself through his right buttock and the calf of his left leg.

The lesson is a simple one; except for unusual circumstances –taking apart a firearm, working a gun's action while lubricating the piece, etc.– nothing is to be in contact with your sidearm's trigger.

*

Magazine fed weapons

First, what is a magazine? It is a spring-loaded container which holds a firearm's ammunition supply. Magazines are frequently referred to by the colloquial term "clip." A clip is, in point of fact, a stamped piece of metal used for the loading of magazines. While that is the correct terminology, unless speaking to a professional firearms instructor, I wouldn't expect the average shooter to differentiate between the terms.

To make a magazine fed firearm safe you MUST first do one of two things;

> Remove the source of the ammunition (the magazine) from the firearm, or,
> Empty the spring-loaded container (an internal magazine, tube magazine, whatever the configuration) of the firearm in which the ammo is located in.
> In either case, this must be done before working the action!

If a pistol magazine is not removed prior to manipulating the gun's action, all the shooter is doing is ejecting the round in the chamber and replacing it with a round from the magazine. Although I have no statistical data on the number of accidents caused by this omission, my empirical observations, and life experience, tell me it's a serious safety issue, causing much unnecessary injury and death each year.

Where are magazines located in firearms if not within the pistol's grip? While I realize this book is about handguns, I thought I might as well offer the information to my readers as to where, in long guns, a person ought to be looking for various weapon magazines.

With any .22 rim fire rifle, if you see a tube visible under the barrel, that is the gun's magazine. Use caution when unloading these firearms. It is not uncommon for a round to "stick" in the tube even after the tube has been "emptied."

Some rim fire rifles have their magazine located in the gun's butt. Normally, turning an exposed knob in the butt stock will permit the tube's removal. The same warning in regard stuck rounds applies to those magazine tubes as well.

Bolt action rifles, of any caliber, often have their ammunition source located directly under the firearm's operating bolt. Sometimes the magazine is an integral part of the gun's mechanism, on occasion the magazine is a separate unit (a box magazine), intended to be removed, loaded and unloaded, independent of the firearm.

Lever action rifles most often have a tube magazine under the barrel. The Savage 99 has an internal rotary magazine in some of its models. Some lever guns also use box removable magazines.

Semi-auto rifles most often utilize box magazines. Some older models held their fixed magazines in a tube underneath the barrel.

There are (many) exceptions for each of these assorted weapon types. Prior to attempting to unload a firearm, it would be prudent to first ask yourself, "Do I know what I'm doing with this firearm?" and, "Am I prepared to take responsibility for the consequences of my actions?"

Here is a clip and a loaded magazine. The clip is used to rapidly insert the rounds into the magazine, most commonly for military applications.

The clip is inserted into a fitting in the rifle and the ammunition is pushed down, with the thumb, in order to load the internal spring- loaded magazine of this military rifle.

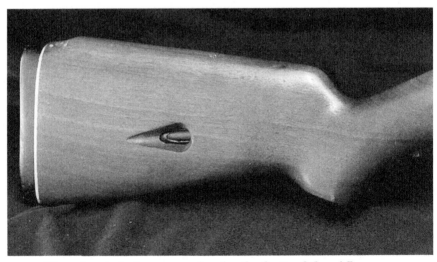

Here is a tubular magazine in the butt of the rifle.

Your firearm's primary safety is your trigger finger. Your secondary safety is the computer between your ears.

Now that you have in your hand an unloaded firearm why is it important to care about where the muzzle is pointing? I mean, the gun is empty, right? Can't hurt anyone, right?

Wrong.

We are all creatures of habit and repetition. Simply stated, if you are in the habit of pointing an unloaded firearm in an unsafe manner, because the gun is "empty," then you will do the very same thing with a loaded firearm. I promise you this is true.

Let me share with you the story of NYPD police firearms instructor Norman (not his real name). As with every police firearms instructor in the department, Norman had been issued a "red-barrel" S&W model 10 revolver. These sidearms were identical to a fully functioning revolver with two exceptions; their firing pins had been removed and their barrels (and sometimes their grip panels as well) were painted bright red. Red barrel guns were the only firearms permitted to be routinely pointed at others for training purposes.

Norman had a habit. As he considered his red barrel revolver little more than a training prop, he used it as a pointer of sorts. When Norman wished to highlight something he was saying, he'd frequently unholster his red barrel gun and wave it around, merrily clicking away on its trigger while he did so. He did this several times a day, for quite a while, until the action became an ingrained habit.

One day Norman and another firearms instructor wanted to look at a used car for sale located near the range. To do this they had to leave the training facility, an over fifty-acre piece of fenced in property which was part of Rodman's Neck in the Bronx. Before leaving the range, it was required that the men, both of course sworn police officers, put their non-functioning revolvers in their lockers and switch to their fully functional handguns, which they did.

As the two headed toward the parking lot, the other instructor decided that he had to relieve himself. He strolled over to a convenient tree and proceeded to do just that. Norman, aware that their hour lunch break time was rapidly dwindling, wished to hurry his friend along. So, as he had done so many times in the past, he pulled out his revolver, pointed it as his buddy, said something to the effect that they had to hurry, and pulled the trigger.

The bullet from his handgun entered his friend's leg. While the wound wasn't a lethal one, it wasn't a particularly good career move for Norman either.

I repeat, you should treat every firearm, loaded or unloaded, with the same degree of respect and caution. There are no different safety rules for the handling of an unloaded firearm as opposed to a loaded gun.

*

The NYPD Firearms and Tactics Section identified the two most common causes of accidental/unintentional discharges as:

> ➤ The improperly "unloaded" firearm, and,
> ➤ the cocked handgun.

It is one of the reasons why, when using either the single-action capable revolver or semi-auto pistol, that the single-action mode of fire during the confusion of a combat confrontation is so hazardous to both the gun's user and those around them. I realize that many handguns designed for service use are either single-action or capable of firing in single-action mode. Some of these handguns are beautifully crafted sidearms and, at least in regard the Browning designed Colt 1911 pattern, have a loyal following.

Be that as it may, I urge the average firearms user to avoid acquiring such a handgun type if the weapon's purpose is for its use in self-defense. Unless an individual is willing to undergo a rather extensive initial training program, with scheduled, periodic, and significant retraining, this type design poses a greater danger to the user, and those around them, than they might wish to admit.

There are many modern sidearms of equal power and similar size that have controls which require far less muscle memory to use properly during an exigent situation. Don't fall prey to peer or hobbyist pressures when deciding on which "serious" handgun to acquire.

*

Toying with the gun

Many years ago, I recall reading some advice in regard who has the "right" to see your firearm. The suggestion was, there were three people who can legitimately ask you to show them your weapon:

> ➢ 1-your military or police superior
> ➢ 2-your firearms instructor
> ➢ 3-your parents

The original wording had "your father" at number three. However, wishing to be thought of as enlightened, I've thrown mom into the mix. For the most part, if anyone asks to see your firearm, you can feel free to decline, with the degree of civility suitable to the moment.

Anytime a person is around firearms good judgment is always needed. Don't permit your handgun to become a casual conversation piece or permit it to be used as a "party favor" when with a group of friends. This warning is particularly true when at a gathering where alcohol is being consumed. It might be wise to avoid having a handgun in your possession under circumstance where it is likely an acquaintance might ask to handle it, which might well place you in an embarrassing social situation.

Alcohol and Firearms

In any discussion regarding firearms safety there are many concerns which are important. This next one is vitally so;

DO NOT HANDLE FIREARMS after consuming alcohol (any amount). This is not a debatable admonition. Alcohol removes inhibition. When around firearms you must be doubly aware of your actions. The mix of this drug (yes, alcohol is a drug) and firearms is lethal. When I say no alcohol, I mean not a glass of sherry, a sip of wine or a taste of beer.

You should not handle a firearm when at a social gathering with others around you consuming alcohol. Furthermore, bars and guns do not mix. Alcohol impairs judgment. What condition would you be in should you actually needed to employ your firearm for its intended purpose after consuming several ounces of alcohol?

Of course, should you be in a bar and a robbery took place, you could be a hero. Or dead.

Some years ago, an off-duty NYPD officer was at a pleasant neighborhood sports bar in a low crime section of the city. He was seated next to a nicely dressed gentleman. The two discussed matters relating to sports for several hours, taking turns buying each other drinks. Later in the evening two men came in and announced a hold-up. The officer slide from his bar stool, reached for his trusty five shot S&W revolver and, as he announced his identity to the robbers, his new found friend in the seat next to him shot him six times with a .45 caliber pistol. You see, the robbery team wasn't just the two men who entered the bar with their guns drawn, but rather consisted of three men. The well-dressed patron was their back-up man.

Although the officer did not die of his wounds, his career as a police officer was over, as the rounds did him crippling damage.

As an aside, robbers are not stupid, just criminal. Back-up robbers working with robbery teams are common. Many pretend to be robbed along with everyone else and stay around to both learn what information the other victims give to the police as well as to give misleading descriptions to the police.

If you think it wise to routinely sit in a bar, armed, while you consume alcohol, I suggest the end result might not be to your liking. Furthermore, in many parts of the country, the consumption of alcohol at a bar or restaurant while carrying a concealed firearm is a violation of law. Don't do it.

*

Some General Firearm Safety Issues

Cleaning firearms and safety

- ➢ No alcohol to be consumed!
- ➢ Work in a quiet area
- ➢ Empty the weapon(s) properly
- ➢ Remove ammunition from the area
- ➢ If the firearm is to be reloaded, immediately put it away for a period of time

Alcohol

If you are in the habit of cleaning your firearms while consuming alcohol you are asking for a serious problem. I am aware that my continued warnings about mixing firearms and alcohol might begin to grate. None the less, I would not be serving your interests if I didn't make the danger of combining the two very, very clear. Some years ago, I saw a scene as to what might happen should you ignore my warnings. This incident took place in the Bronx, New York, in the mid-1970s. A man, after an evening drinking at a local bar, came home and decided it would be a good time to clean his lever action deer rifle. He had a few more beers (three open bottles were around him) and began to work on his gun. Regrettably, he did not clear the weapon properly. His daughter, a child of around six or seven, woke up and came out to say hello to daddy. She stepped over to her father and pressed the gun's trigger while the muzzle was pointed at the man's chest.

It was a bloody mess.

I apologize if it seems like I'm harping on this no alcohol issue. Do trust me, it's important or I wouldn't go on and on about it.

Quiet area

You want to be away from distractions. No yelling kids, dealing with household matters with the spouse or other distractions should be taking place near you. Not a big deal, it's just safer to work on a firearm under serene conditions.

Empty the weapon properly

I've gone over the correct protocol for unloading firearms earlier. Your responsibility is to exercise this knowledge now. Don't take a shortcut. Do it correctly.

Remove all ammunition from the area

Once again, I would like to assure the reader that this is something I do, religiously, and it is something you ought to do as well. Remember, the very act of cleaning a handgun will require you to manipulate the weapon in ways that might be deemed unsafe under other circumstances. You do not want the possibility that a live round might somehow have managed to find its way into a firearm's mechanism when you least expect it.

If reloading the firearm, put it away!

As I mentioned above, when cleaning a firearm, by necessity, you are handling the gun in unsafe ways; working the trigger in order to disperse lubricant, looking down the muzzle to check for cleanliness, etc. Once the gun is clean, and you feel it necessary to immediately load the piece, you must –and I mean MUST– put the firearm out of your immediate reach for a solid half hour or so.

Your goal is to get your mind out of "Gun Cleaning Mode" and back into "Loaded Firearm Mode."

*

Dry-Firing

Dry-firing a handgun is an excellent way to both practice your skills as well as maintain proficiency with your sidearm. I hope it's by now obvious to you that, prior to engaging in such activity, you take the proper safety precautions; dry-fire your handgun in a safe, quiet area after first ensuring the sidearm is unloaded safely.

As when you've finished cleaning the handgun, once the dry-firing exercise is over, put the gun away for a period of time prior to reloading it. This is to permit your mind to get out of the "unloaded gun / dry-firing" mode and into the "loaded gun" state of mind. Again, this is an important warning, not to be ignored.

*

Weapons around untrained children and immature adults

Considerations:

> - To train or not to train children?
> - Hide your gun/s or don't hide them?
>   (remember peer pressure)
> - Immature/unstable adults

When there are firearms in a household along with youngsters, at some point in the life of a family there is the conundrum as to whether or not to train the children within the home in their safe handling. If they should be trained, at what age? Since each family is different, I can't offer up a definitive answer for you in this matter. Having stated that, I do believe it's an important issue that requires some serious thought and discussion on the part of the parents in regard how to handle the matter.

One dilemma you face is that regardless of the degree of maturity on the part of your children, they are terribly prone to succumb to peer pressure. So, if your children's friends are aware there are firearms in the home, and circumstances are such that a group of children are alone in the home playing, it is very difficult for one child to withstand the nagging of another child when, after initially denying them access to dad's handgun, the other child starts on your child with taunts of, "You afraid? Common, you're just being yellow!"

My instinct is, depending on the personalities of the children involved as well as the home's family dynamic, it is best to train them in the proper and safe handling of firearms, with a careful and deliberate emphasis on the need to keep other children away from any firearms in the home. This admonition should include instructing the children that if they found themselves at a friend's home, and the offer to show them "dad's gun" came up, they must, immediately, vacate the premises. Tough for kids to do, but with potentially lethal consequences if not done.

As far as hiding your handgun/s from the kids, really? Don't you remember your childhood days? Was there a place within your home that you didn't get into at one time or another? The bottom line here is, quite simply, the only way to secure firearms from one's children is in a very secure locked container or gun vault.

Immature/unstable adults

Simply stated, some people should not be permitted near firearms. You know who they are within your family's structure. This can be a difficult situation to deal with. You must exercise good judgment in regard who has access to your firearms. If you hand over a firearm to an untrained individual, or otherwise permit them access to your firearms, you will be held responsible for the consequences.

*

How a child discharges a double-action revolver

A police firearms instructor I worked with, Wally Ostermyer, told me the following tale. A police officer assigned to a northern Manhattan precinct came home after completing his midnight tour of duty. After placing his gun and gun belt high up in his bedroom closet, he went to bed. Once asleep his six year old son got a chair, climbed up and found of his dad's revolver.

When Wally and his partner arrived at the apartment the father was sitting at the kitchen table, his head in his hands, not saying a word. His wife, hysterically crying, was in another room. Wally stepped into the bedroom. As he described the scene to me, pieces of the child's brains were splattered all over the ceiling, the small body lay on the floor.

You see, although a child does not have sufficient strength in the trigger finger to discharge a double-action revolver, there is another way for them to operate such a handgun in order to cause the gun to go off. They use their thumbs. And, upon placing the thumbs on a handgun's trigger, the muzzle of the weapon is naturally aimed at the head.

You cannot make a double-action service type revolver any safer without detracting from its primary virtue – that of it being ready for instantaneous use. This means, simply put, that untrained people, and little children, cannot be permitted to have access to such firearms, or a tragedy will occur.

Safeguarding Firearms from Loss and Theft

Loss

The single safest place for a handgun to be is on your person, in a well-designed holster. Avoid inside the pants holsters which use a metal clip to secure the gun to your waist. Handguns are not infrequently lost because of this design. The gun (while still in its holster) may tumble out of the pants when exiting a car, jogging or engaging in strenuous activity.

I recall once, when assigned to the 8th Narcotics District in the Bronx, New York, my team was taking down a door pursuant to a search warrant. One of the guys on the ram (the "key to the city") was wearing this type of holster. As the officer was battering on the door his holster, gun still in it, fell out of his pants. I grabbed the weapon from off the floor and jammed it in my pocket just as the door popped open and we all entered with our guns drawn. Except for that officer on the ram who, while in the middle of executing a warrant at a known drug dealer's location, burst into the place unarmed! The only good thing about such holster designs is, they are cheap. In this case, you get what you pay for.

Do not carry a handgun in a bag, envelope, lunch box, sack or any other container not attached to your body *(this includes pocketbooks!!)*. Doing so invites loss of the weapon. Furthermore, it is very easy to unintentionally leave your "package" where you did not intend! Many a handgun has been found by a New York City cab driver in the back seat of the cab! I am confident in stating that, if you routinely carry your handgun in a container not attached to your body, you <u>will</u> lose it! I'm willing to bet a large cup of coffee and a donut on the matter.

Pocketbooks are a particular issue that needs to be addressed. Too many women carry their personal protection handguns in their purses. It's a terrible idea. This is a case where the folks who carry their handguns in their purses believe they are going about armed, when in fact they will have no ready access to their handguns in an actual emergency. When discussing the matter with my female students I put forth a few rhetorical questions;

Q~ Where do women keep their valuables?

A~ In their purses.

Q~ What are muggers looking for?

A~ Valuables.

Q~ How do muggers routinely avail themselves of a woman's valuables?

A~ By snatching the purse.

Q~ In a tug-of-war between the average woman and a healthy twenty-something year old street robber, who do they think will prevail? And just how much protection do they seriously think a little handgun will be during this brawl while it is sitting in a purse?

I recall talking with the husband of an older, frail woman, who had been the victim of a recent mugging (a purse snatch). He wanted her to go armed and thought it would be a good idea for her to carry her handgun in her pocketbook. How was she robbed, I asked? His answer, "A thief grabbed her purse, violently yanked it from her and ran off with it." I asked him how a handgun sitting inside that pocketbook would have been of any utility under those circumstances? He got the point.

*

Theft

There is no foolproof method for keeping a firearm out of the hands of a professional burglar. The most secure method of protection in the home is a good quality gun vault which is securely bolted to the building's structure. While it is true that you cannot protect yourself against all burglaries, most burglars are in and out of the home in five minutes. The criminals are mostly after money, jewelry and credit cards.

None the less, given enough time, even a well-made safe can be defeated. It's just lots tougher to do.

At home it is generally best to conceal your firearms in obscure places. Firearms left exposed in a glass gun-case isn't a good idea. If at all possible, lock your firearms up in a secure container. This may prevent their discovery and the unwanted removal of the firearm. This also keeps the firearm/s away from untrained family members.

Don't ever try and "hide" a firearm (or anything of value) in a dresser drawer. This is the first place a burglar goes to when searching the home. Burglars don't gently rummage through drawers. Rather, they rip them from the bureau and scatter their contents on the floor or nearby bed.

A burglarized home looks like the proverbial tornado had been through the place.

Hiding a gun among the family's dirty clothes is not a particularly good spot either. Burglars will sometimes go there to seek out an old pillow case to carry away their loot.

The bottom line is, don't make it easy for the wrong people to find your firearms; if you don't have a secure safe consider using an empty detergent box under the sink or a hollowed out book and certainly don't display firearms openly in the home. Moreover, you should keep firearms separate from jewelry and money.

*

Safeguarding firearms while away from home

Don't advertise or otherwise draw attention to the fact that you have a firearm. Don't display an NRA sticker or any other indication on your car that you are interested in firearms, especially if circumstances are such that you must, from time to time, store a handgun in the vehicle (as when entering a facility which prohibits the carrying of concealed weapons).

Understand, an auto is a terrible place to keep a firearm, especially under the driver's seat. It takes only seconds for an experienced thief to gain access to your auto's interior. If you feel there will be circumstances where you have no viable alternative but to keep your firearm in an unattended vehicle, there are small, reasonably robust gun safes made just for that purpose. Buy one and utilize it.

A motel or hotel room is a poor place to store a firearm. Strangers routinely access your room (for daily cleaning and sometimes general maintenance). Some hotels have secure areas to store valuables. This might be an option, just don't advertise the fact that the motel is storing a gun for you!

When on vacation, if you know you are going swimming, or will be at a picnic or involved in active sports, think ahead as to whether or not you should have a firearm with you. Use mature judgment.

*

A word about blanks; they are lethal at close range and have caused the death of more than a few people. They can also damage your hearing as well as do significant damage to the eyes. While it is true that blank cartridges have no "bullets," the gas escaping from the gun's muzzle is what causes the loud bang and is traveling at several thousand feet per second. If there is a paper wad covering the cartridge's muzzle, that very light material, traveling at very, very high velocity, will, at close range, penetrate a human's skull.

Use caution around blanks, they are not to be toyed with!

Lowering the hammer on a live round

I debated whether to include this material under this chapter or within the Manual of Arms chapter but, as it directly relates to the safe handling of the double-action revolver, decided to place it here.

The average, untrained person, when lowering the hammer of a double-action revolver, almost always does it in an unsafe manner. The drill, as

I've observed it so many times, is for the person, with finger on the trigger, to use the shooting hand thumb to hold back the hammer, pull on the trigger, and then ease the hammer forward, finger still pressing on the trigger. There's a better, and far safer way, to perform this task, developed by the NYPD after a few "incidents."

Procedure

The admonition, to keep one's finger off the trigger until about to fire, is the primary method of insuring this operation is performed safely.

Although the operation sounds complex, when it's broken down into individual actions it is a simple one to perform:

While holding your cocked revolver in the shooting hand, with your shooting hand thumb firmly on the hammer;

1. Ensure your finger is off the trigger and the revolver is pointed in a safe direction,
2. make a fist with your non-shooting hand (really, this is not an option. Doing so keeps fingers away from the gun's muzzle, especially with short barrel revolvers.).
3. Place the thumb of the non-shooting hand between the hammer and the frame, and,
4. with the thumb of the shooting hand, gently pull back on the hammer.
   (until the hammer is safely lowered your shooting hand thumb **does not** leave the hammer spur!)
5. At this time, place your shooting hand trigger finger on the trigger.
6. Put pressure on the trigger, at the same time easing the hammer forward.
7. As the hammer comes closer to the frame, remove your finger from the trigger and move your non-shooting hand thumb out of the way of the hammer and frame.

8. Continue to ease the hammer all the way onto the frame (Remember, *your finger is not on the trigger!!*)

You've successfully and safely lowered the hammer on a live round. The process is a simple one to execute properly and virtually precludes the possibility of an accidental discharge during its commission. I urge you to learn how to perform this maneuver and use it every time you need to lower the hammer on a loaded revolver.

*

The last thought I wish to leave you with in regard the safe handling of firearms is, when you are around weapons you absolutely must ask yourself this question;

If there is an accidental discharge, who will be held responsible??

*

Ear and Eye Safety Equipment

As I am writing this section, I hear the sound of the ocean in my ears. The problem is, I'm not near the beach. I have tinnitus, or ringing in the ears. Twenty-four hours a day, every day, the noise is there. When I first began shooting there were no readily available ear-protectors out there. Sometime we stuck empty shell casings in our ear canals (a pointless exercise), or a bit of cotton. Even if some protection existed, peer pressure was to man-up and just deal with the loud noise of the gun fire. Well, there was a price to pay for that ignorance and bravado. Understand, just a single loud noise can cause irreparable damage to the delicate nerves in the ear.

Prolonged exposure to firearms noise will cause a reduction in hearing acuity. This is not debatable. This loss of hearing will generally take place at the frequency level of the normal human voice. A person with hearing disability will hear pieces of words. Hearing loss is insidious, as it generally takes place over a number of years of exposure to loud noises. Firearms Instructors are particularly prone to this disability.

Muff type protectors are the most efficient means to protect one's hearing. This is because much noise comes in through a small bone situated behind the ear. There are many muff-type electronic ear protectors now available which I've found to be very useful. With them you can hear, or even enhance, normal sounds around you yet these muffs will still protect you from the damaging noise of a discharging firearm. They are a worthwhile investment if you intend to do any serious shooting.

Earplug protection if OK is no other type of hearing protection is available. There are a number of high quality disposable protectors out there, plus many non-disposable versions. It would be wise to research your options carefully (the higher the noise reduction rating attained by a given sound protection device the better) and purchase the protectors well before you will need them. I keep several good quality disposable type protectors salted away in various pieces of shooting gear, just in case of need.

*

Eye protection

Guns <u>do</u> blow up. Cartridges do, from time to time, allow high pressure gases, plus bits of the casing, to come back to hit the shooter in the face. You must –really, really must– wear eye-protection when firing a gun. Some considerations;

> ➤ Even when operating correctly revolvers will sometimes spit lead and burnt/unburnt powder from between the cylinder and barrel throat gap, causing a very real hazard to the eyes. On rare (very rare) occasions, should a revolver blow up, to those standing to either side of the shooter the gun then acts like a hand grenade.
> ➤ Semi-auto pistols eject hot brass, sometimes straight back at the shooter's face.

➢ A rifle or shotgun contains tens of thousands of pounds of pressure upon firing. This pressure sits right by the shooter's face. In the event of an explosion blindness, unless wearing proper eye protection, is a very real risk.

During the routine and normal firing of firearms, powder, lead and brass particles do, from time to time, get blown back onto the face of the shooter. Keep in mind that upon discharge a firearm routinely generates between 20,000 and 40,000 pounds of pressure per square inch, and if a long arm this is happening only inches from your face.

A firearm is not a sealed container. Material is routinely ejected from out of the muzzle, from between the barrel throat and from the end of the cylinder, as well as from a pistol's ejection port. On occasion something unwanted bounces back from downrange. If the object hits you in the leg, you might get a welt, if the object strikes your unprotected eye, you could be in the market for a tin cup.

Many years ago, when assigned to the NYPD Firearms and Tactics Section, one of my tasks was to be in charge of Research and Testing. One day, by myself, I was running a test on some old bullet resistant vests. At this particular section of the range there was a Plexiglas shield with a hole cut in it intended to be used under such circumstances. As no one else was nearby, and I wasn't about to perform any unusual or particularly dangerous test, for a moment I considered not using this safety barrier. But I did use it. Within a few rounds of my starting the test one of the projectiles bounced off the object I was shooting at and stuck the barrier with a loud bang, right where my leg would have been. The round, firing an expanding projectile, hit with such force that it flattened out completely on the Plexiglas. I have no doubt that bullet would have gone deeply into my leg.

Wear eye and ear protection at all times. It makes no sense not to do so.

Lead Poisoning

If you're an active shooter, spend a good deal of time at firing ranges, handload, pick up brass or cast your own projectiles, it would be most prudent of you to have a reasonable concern in regard the potential for coming down with lead poisoning. While lead (a heavy metal) is a most useful material, the problem of humans being poisoned by this metal has been with us for thousands of years. Greeks and Romans were victims of lead poisoning due to the construction of their pipes, food jars and jugs being made of lead and leaded-glass. Shipbuilders from the 1st Century had similar issues.

Lead which gets into the blood system, destroys red blood cells and bone, causing brain, kidney and nervous system damage. Early stages of the poisoning are curable. When the poison gets into the bone the damage is irreversible. Children are far more susceptible to lead poisoning than adults. Children who eat lead paint absorb between 60~70% of the lead while an adult will absorb perhaps 5% of that metal.[4]

There are many sources of lead exposure beside firearms use. These include:

Occupational

- Construction workers
- Steel welders
- Bridge reconstruction workers
- Firing range instructors and cleaners
- Painters
- Remodelers and refinishers
- Foundry workers
- Scrap metal recyclers
- Auto repairers
- Cable splicers

Hobbyists

- ➢ Casting bullets or fishing sinkers
- ➢ Home remodeling
- ➢ Target shooting at firing ranges
- ➢ Lead soldering
- ➢ Auto repair
- ➢ Stained glass making
- ➢ Glazed pottery making

Sources of lead at the shooting range[5]

- ➢ Lead compounds are often utilized in cartridge primers (lead styphnate). Upon firing the round the confined lead becomes airborne. We absorb this material through breathing, ingestion and absorption
- ➢ Lead bullets (when we handle them)
- ➢ Lead bullet vaporization and splintering as it passes through the barrel after being fired (again, through breathing, ingestion and absorption)
- ➢ Fragmentation of the bullet against the target and backstop (the material becomes airborne)
- ➢ Picking up spent cases from the range floor (simply handling the brass transfers lead to the fingers)

Lead collects on the fingers and can be ingested during eating and smoking in a number of ways. These include breathing it in, ingestion through handling food and other objects with contaminated fingers and through skin absorption. Even if they were aware that their fingers had come into contact with lead particulate matter, people routinely and without conscious thought place fingers by their lips and mouth area or rub their eyes.

How can exposure to lead be minimized at the shooting range?

> Better range ventilation decreases the risk of lead poisoning. Outdoor ranges hold less of an issue in this area than indoor ranges.

> Copper-covered (jacketed) bullets reduce the risk of lead poisoning. Some indoor ranges require Totally Metal Jacketed (TMJ) rounds for this reason. Such rounds leave no lead exposed to the air, as the projectile's lead is encapsulated within its jacket. Some ranges ban lead projectiles (and rounds containing lead primer compounds) altogether.

> When shooting outdoors avoid shooting on days when the wind is blowing toward you.

> Limit the time you shoot on a busy range to minimize exposure to second hand lead.

> Do not eat or smoke while shooting. Wash your hands after you shoot.

> Don't rub your eyes or touch your mouth at the shooting range.

> Change and wash your clothing immediately after shooting.

> If you use the restroom at the range, wash your hands first. Lead can be easily absorbed through body parts other than the hands.

Lead poisoning from handling ammunition

Handling rounds of ammunition that contain jacketed bullets are not a concern in regard lead poisoning. Ammunition with exposed lead bullets must be handled more cautiously. This includes .22 rimfire rounds, almost all of which use exposed lead projectiles. After handling ammunition which exposes you to lead you must wash your hands.

Lead poisoning from gun cleaning

Much of the residue on the gun and in the bore most probably contains lead. When you use gun cleaning solvents, which are designed to break-down and clean out this material, you increase your risk of becoming exposed to unwanted amounts of lead. Therefore, it makes good sense, where possible, to put on protective ("surgical") gloves when cleaning your weapons. Not only will you protect yourself from an unnecessary risk of lead contamination, but many solvents are caustic and can cause irritation to the skin. After each gun cleaning session wash your hands.

Lead poisoning from reloading ammunition

Reloading of lead bullets holds the same risk as handling lead ammunition. The handling and cleaning of spent cases is another source of lead. The dust from the tumbling material used to clean the brass cases may contain high levels of lead. Tumbling should best be done outdoors or at least with an eye toward minimizing your contact with any fumes coming out of the process. Obviously, the medium used in the tumbler contains lead dust and should be handled with care.

Signs and symptoms of lead poisoning

Lead poisoning is an insidious illness. Some signs that you may have ingested too much of this heavy metal might be fatigue, headache, uneasy stomach, sleeplessness, irritability or nervousness, having a metallic taste in the mouth, poor appetite or reproductive problems.

Later signs and symptoms of the problem include; aches/pains in the stomach, memory problems, headaches and dizziness, anemia, constipation, muscle and joint pains, nausea, weak wrists or ankles, weight loss and kidney problems.

Lead contamination might impact other members of your family. If you don't remember to wash after shooting, when you get home and play with the kids you could well be shifting the risk over to them.

Firearms Safety References

[1]Seedman, Albert, *Chief!*, Arthur Fields Books, Inc. New York, The Belt Parkway Case, p. 9

[2]Mail Online at:

http://www.dailymail.co.uk/news/article-1240433/Boy-killed-bullet-fired-2-miles-away.html#ixzz1qIIwG2zN

[3]Huffington Post at:

http://www.huffingtonpost.com/2011/12/21/amish-girl-shooting-gun-cleaning_n_1162704.html

[4]Lifescript at:

http://www.lifescript.com/health/a-z/conditions_a-z/conditions/l/lead_poisoning.aspx?gclid=CIud44TKiLMCFY-d4AodJF8AVA&trans=1&du=1&ef_id=UGYaUQAARx27vCKl%3a20121017173031%3as

[5]PoliceOne.com: *Get the Lead Out: Reducing Lead Exposure on the Gun Range*

http://www.policeone.com/columnists/lom/articles/1190023-Get-the-lead-out-Reducing-lead-exposure-on-the-gun-range/

Cleaning the Handgun

(Less is sometimes more…)

There are many different, and valid, approaches to firearms maintenance. When with NYPD's Firearms & Tactics Unit I was told by a department gunsmith that from time to time senior officers would come to them with their old service revolvers and complain that the handguns' actions were "stiff." Sure, they were stiff, having the better part of twenty years of old dried-out oil gumming up their inner works!

When that happened, the gunsmith would take the revolver in (back in those days officers were only permitted revolvers for duty use) and send the officer on his way to continue the day's training with a department issued loaner gun. The gunsmith would then remove the revolver's wood grips, and stick the entire gun in a can of solvent. Around lunch time they'd remove the handgun from the solvent and hang it over the can on a stout wire, permitting the residual solvent, along with whatever detritus it removed from the guts of the handgun, to drip out of the revolver. Shortly before the end of the training day they'd replace the grips. The officer, at the end of the day, upon retrieving the handgun, would try the action and inevitably exclaim in joy as to what a great job the gunsmiths had done in "fixing" that revolver!

What should the goal be when "cleaning" a handgun? The answer is relatively simple; we need to ensure the handgun remains in serviceable condition and that it will function reliably when needed. If the handgun is made of ferrous metal, protecting the gun's surface from rust is also important.

We perform the above by removing burnt and unburned powder particles around the area of the action as well as inside the barrel. Sometimes it is also necessary to remove lead fouling from inside the barrel and around the operating mechanism, although this is becoming less common as the use of jacketed rounds of ammunition becomes more and more the norm.

Cleaning a handgun does not mean it is necessary (or even desirable) to bring the handgun to as close to pristine condition as possible, by removing every speck of powder, lead and other bits of fouling present. You can get carried away with the cleaning process and put more wear on your firearm by excessive and overly exuberant cleaning than by simply giving it a relatively thorough yet modest going over. It's a balance. Let's discuss it a bit before we get into the actual how-to of maintaining your sidearm.

My rule of thumb is, if the firearm is a primary personal defense handgun, then I clean it after each use. If it's a sporting sidearm, and depending on the purpose it is to be put, every few hundred rounds is a reasonable amount of usage between cleanings. Obviously, if you plan on putting a handgun away for an extended period of time, then a good cleaning would be in order.

One last thing. While I enjoy the act of cleaning my handguns I never touch any firearm if I've consumed ANY amount of alcohol. That means even a single beer. Once the alcohol comes out, the firearms had better be put away. This is an inviolate rule. Disobey it at your peril.

*

Tools: Supplies needed

I suppose one of the simpler ways of acquiring the basic and necessary implements required for the cleaning of firearms is by purchasing one of the many small gun-cleaning kits put out by various manufacturers. Such a kit would certainly serve as a good basis for your collection of "stuff" that you will find useful when working on your handguns. Keeping this in mind, I would like to offer some other suggestions for you to consider:

Acquire a few cleaning rods if possible. True, you only need one. But if you're a shooter, having several rods, each holding a different cleaning brush and accessory in your favorite calibers, can prove to be very handy. It's your call. There are cleaning rods that are made with a ball bearing in the handle, permitting the rod to rotate as you push it in and out of the gun. Some folks like this setup. I have lots of rods from different manufacturers and I can't really tell much of a difference between those with such a design and conventional rods. At any rate, in addition, you should purchase or acquire:

> Solvent

Used to break up burned and unburned particles of powder, Hoppe's #9 has been around for many years and, in my experience, works just fine. Just don't use Hoppe's #9 on nickel plated handguns (it destroys the nickel finish if left on for too long a time). Should you prefer to use another kind of solvent on your firearm, there are dozens of other brands and types out there, each with their advocates who swear on the superiority of their choices.

> Lubricants

Break-Free CLP is very good. Some folks like Mobil 1 (5w-30 weight synthetic motor oil) and claim it works just fine. Any name-brand gun oil should serve as a suitable lubricant for your handgun, assuming routine maintenance is performed on a regular basis. Extreme environments often mean non-standard lubricants are in order. Our guys out in the Middle East seem to have to deal with particularly insidious fine sand and have come up with their own set of solutions to deal with their unique dilemma.

A needle-nose oil container is very handy for properly placing lubrication on those parts requiring same. Less oil in the mechanism is better than too much. Whatever lubricant you choose, do try to use a needle-nose applicator. This tends to keep you from over oiling your handguns. Please remember, firearms cleaning isn't an "oil and grease job" as done on your cars. Over lubricating a handgun is a very poor idea.

➤ Grease

Some folks also find use for a good quality gun grease (best if held in a container with a syringe-type thin nosed applicator attached) which they prefer to use over normal oil lubricants on the rails and other parts of their pistols. Others recommend a high quality, high-temperature automotive wheel bearing grease, which is cheap, easily obtained and very likely will serve you well.

➤ Patches

Cotton is best. I like the military surplus ones. Once found, buy a bunch and cut to size as needed. If no patches are available, cut up some old underwear (yes, I know, they're the most comfortable ones). I suggest you do not try and continue to use the underwear once it is put to this alternate purpose. As with military patches, cut your underwear patch sizes to match the caliber of the handgun being maintained. For my .22s, in lieu of patches I often use Q-Tips to clean my bores and chambers.

➤ An old toothbrush (or just borrow your spouse's…)

After being dipped in solvent a toothbrush is very useful for getting into a firearm's tight spots.

➤ Small cup to hold solvent

I use a small shallow glass cup (perhaps it's an ashtray, I'm not sure) in which I pour my solvent. It prevents me from having the potential mess of me tipping over the whole bottle of Hoppe's #9.

➤ Rag/s

You can never have enough rags. Once again, old and worn underwear shirts serve admirably in this role. I prefer my rags to be grungy with old gun oil, and assign value to them accordingly.

> ➤ Bristle brush/s

Bristle brushes come in many styles and are made of several materials, including; nylon, brass or steel. I have no set preference, although, out of perhaps excessive caution I do tend to avoid the steel versions. Do remember, once you have inserted a brush into the bore of a firearm you MUST push the brush completely through before reversing its direction or you will instantly destroy that brush!

As an aside, please go easy with the brushing part of cleaning if using a steel brush.

> ➤ An old (worn out) bristle brush for use with patches

You certainly can use a jag or a slotted end-piece to hold your patches. It is simply that I've found that an old, worn out bristle brush ensures excellent uniform contact between the patch and the gun's bore.

> ➤ Slab of cardboard or similar material to work on

Gun cleaning can be messy and some of the solvents damaging to certain household materials and table tops. This little caution goes a long way to protect whatever surface you opt to work on (such as mom's kitchen table).

> ➤ "Rubber" (surgical) gloves

Good for people who have sensitive skin. Some gun cleaning chemicals can be pretty strong. I find that Hoppe's #9 (a great gun cleaning solvent) causes the skin on my fingers to split open. Therefore, I use gloves when cleaning firearms. Your pharmacy should have such gloves in stock. A little larger than you require is better than a size a bit too small.

> ➤ Dental picks and tools

Ask your dentist for some of his old worn out dental tools. I've also seen such tools for sale at gun shows. Very useful for getting into tight places and scrapping lead away from various parts of a revolver's frame, especially near the forcing cone.

> A bib

When you clean your handgun you will undoubtedly splatter "stuff" all over the place, particularly the front of your body. After destroying a number of perfectly good shirts I decided that, in this matter, discretion was the better part of valor. Thus, I now wear a bib when cleaning my firearms. Plus, when I put on my bib, I've been told I look adorable.

*

I've found that putting all my cleaning supplies in a single container makes my life easier. There are many small plastic tool boxes that are suitable for such use. A fisherman's tackle box, with its various compartments, should prove to be a very practical holder of gun cleaning implements.

For those of you with enough space in the home I urge you consider using a single small drawer for such purposes. Doing so really makes gun cleaning a much simpler chore. In my case I'm fortunate to have a quiet place where I can clean my firearms, located by an old bureau. My gun cleaning materials are in one drawer, so, once my bib goes on and a square of cardboard placed in front of me, I'm in business.

Safety!

Ensure that the firearm to be cleaned is unloaded! Unload the firearm properly! Check it twice to make sure it's empty! Way too many folks have had "gun cleaning" accidents for you to ignore this warning!

If it's a semi-automatic pistol, before working the action of the handgun you must *first remove the source of its ammunition* (the magazine)!

Whatever the type handgun, remove all ammunition from the area where cleaning is to take place! Again, this is non-negotiable. The reason is simple; in a moment it will be necessary for you to handle your handgun in what would otherwise be an unsafe manner. Gremlins exist which will conspire to insert a live round in a firearm you believe is unloaded. Don't help the little dears.

*

The Fundamentals

Blued/Stainless/Polymer Framed Firearms:

There is nothing quite as handsome as a finely blued firearm. Regrettably, bluing, which is itself a rusting process, does very little to protect a ferrous metal firearm's surface from rust.

In order to protect a blued sidearm something must come between the salt and moisture on your skin and the metal of the firearm. Furthermore, a blued metal firearm in a high salt air environment, or when worn next to the body, requires daily maintenance (at minimum a wipe down with an oily rag) in order to protect the firearm's surface. Indeed, under certain extreme circumstances such maintenance should be done more than once a day.

A light oil coating is better than nothing, but to really preserve a blued metal firearm you'll need a more robust and heavier viscosity protectant. RIG (Rust Inhibiting Grease) has been around for generations and I've found it to be most useful. I have no doubt other good quality firearms greases and metal protectors will serve as well, I just have no direct experience with them.

Stainless handguns are inherently more resistant to rust and corrosion then their blued relatives. It is possible to cause rust to form on the surface of a stainless handgun, it simply takes some effort to accomplish this task.

Polymer (plastic) handguns are likely the most rust and corrosion resistant models available. Their plastic parts are, for all practical purposes, inert and immune to body salt corrosion concerns. Modern handguns often have chemical protections (Tennifer and Melonite –salt bath nitriding– come to mind) deposited on their metal surfaces which go a long way to ensure they remain rust and corrosion free. Having said that, I continue to wipe down my polymer framed handguns metal slides. Old habits die hard, and, anyway, it can't hurt.

Semi-automatic pistols

First, properly UNLOAD the handgun. As I've stated several times, remove the magazine (your source of ammunition) from the handgun before manipulating the gun's action in any way. Your finger should be nowhere near the handgun's trigger at this time.

Remove all ammo from the area where the gun is to be cleaned.

Disassemble the semi-auto handgun into its basic components, generally its receiver or frame, slide and barrel. You know how to do this because; you've taken prior training specific to this model pistol, you've read the gun's manual, cover to cover, and you've watched YouTube videos on the internet showing you how this is properly and safely accomplished.

Because there are numerous pistol models out there I can't begin to tell you how to properly take-apart your pistol. If you purchased your handgun new, it came with a manual. Read it. Otherwise check out the internet for information on your handgun's take-down procedures. YouTube is a good resource for many firearm models, particularly the 1911 platform. Only take-down the pistol to the extent required for cleaning. You're not a gunsmith. Furthermore, I was quite serious about you taking professional firearms training which is relevant to your model handgun. Would you expect a person to operate a car, aircraft, motorcycle or other potentially dangerous piece of equipment without such training?

Bore and barrel

Place a bore brush of the correct diameter on your rod, dip it in solvent and run the brush through from the chamber end of the barrel. The reason a bore brush should, when possible, go in from the chamber end is to protect the muzzle end of the barrel from undue wear and abuse. The bore brush MUST go all the way through the bore before pulling if out. Failure to do that will destroy a new brush.

After brushing your handgun's chamber with solvent, a clean dry patch should be used to remove residual liquids. Your chamber should be clean and DRY. No lubrication or other fluid is desirable in a pistol's chamber. You risk contaminating the ammunition as well as causing a malfunction.

You want the inside of the barrel to be clean, with a light coat of protective oil on the rifled portion and just a dry surface in the chamber. There are two reasons you want the chamber dry;

1. So as not to contaminate the cartridge's primer with solvent or whatever other chemical you've used in the cleaning process, and,

2. To prevent the discharged cartridge case from acting as an hydraulic piston. It should remain unmoved in the pistol's chamber during the initial phase of discharge (the term is obduration). This is one of the purposes a cartridge serves. Cartridges are designed to act as a gas seal until pulled out of their chamber by the pistol's extractor at the appropriate time in the handgun's normal firing cycle.

*

Slide

Use your toothbrush dipped lightly in solvent and scrub around the inside of the slide. Keep excessive amounts of the liquid from getting into the inner workings of the slide (such as the firing pin channel or the place where the extractor sits).

*

Frame

Use your old toothbrush, dipped in solvent, and scrub the visible areas of the frame. Then take a rag and remove as much of the gunk and solvent as possible. A Q-Tip might prove useful in getting into some of the narrow places around the frame.

*

Revolvers

Properly UNLOAD the handgun. Open (or remove the cylinder if a single-action handgun) and clear away all ammunition from the work area. As with the semi-auto pistol, you will be manipulating your sidearm in ways contrary to normal and safe handling protocols.

Dip your old toothbrush into your solvent and brush around the outside of the firearm, near the throat of the barrel and anywhere you see burned and unburned powder particles. This includes the front and rear of your cylinder as well as the front and rear of the barrel. Let the solvent remain for a few minutes while you continue cleaning the revolver.

Run your bristle brush, dipped in solvent, through each of the cylinder's chambers, then through the barrel from the muzzle. There are bore snakes available that permit cleaning from the throat end of the revolver's barrel should you wish to procure one.

Your chambers should be clean and DRY. No lubrication is desirable in the chambers of a revolver.

At this time take a clean, dry patch and run it through each of the revolver's chambers. I generally run a few patches through my revolver's chambers. Often the last patch used is pretty clean. I put some lubricant, gun grease or oil on it and run it through the otherwise clean barrel. You want clean, dry chambers so that upon discharge your cartridge case remains firmly in place. You <u>DO NOT</u> want the cartridge cases in your chambers to act as hydraulic pistons. Lubrication in the chamber may permit a fired cartridge case to move forcefully to the rear, pushing against the recoil plate of the handgun and, over time, possibly causing the handgun to malfunction.

Make sure you remove all possible debris from under your extractor, the piece that pushes the spent rounds from their chambers (sometimes referred to as the "star," sometime as an "ejector". The name of the part varies with the manufacturer.). If there is debris (say a broken-off bristle from a bristle brush) stuck under this part the cylinder might not close, or, it might close but be very difficult to open.

If you wish, place a single drop of oil into the handgun's mechanism. Yes, that was one drop. Period. Pull the trigger through a dozen or so times in order to spread the lubrication around.

Wipe down the outside of the handgun with a rag.

Years past a trick used to ensure lead was removed from a revolver's bore was to fill the bore, plugged at one end, with mercury. The heavy metal was left in the bore overnight. As mercury amalgamates with lead it was an excellent method to ensure a clean bore. I mention this only because someone might recommend you use this process. Although I possess some mercury, I've found other ways to get the lead out of my revolvers bores. Mercury dropped on the floor is a mess to clean up and the stuff is quite toxic. Please don't use any for this purpose.

*

.22 Rimfire Handguns:

There are two main .22 caliber handguns; those for the .22 Long Rifle cartridge, and those for the .22 Magnum round. The magnum cartridge generally uses a jacketed projectile, which offers little or no protection for the bore of the handgun after firing. The .22 Long Rifle generally uses an outside lubricated projectile and thus serves to give the bore of the handgun some protection from corrosion after the gun has been used.

I clean the bores of my .22s every few hundred rounds. If you don't clean your pistols then I think you'll find that, especially with your semi-automatic .22 handguns, the burned and unburned powder particles collecting in and around the pistol's action will begin to cause malfunctions.

The problem part of the .22 Long Rifle revolver, in my experience, is in the cylinder's chambers. Depending on the round used (some brands are lots dirtier than others) you might have to run a solvent soaked Q-Tip through each chamber a number of times during a shooting session as the rounds become harder and harder to insert into the chambers, and even more difficult to eject without a solid rap to the ejection rod. In my shooting bag I keep a small bottle of Hoppe's #9, plus a goodly supply of Q-Tips just for that purpose.

I clean the bores of my .22s (both magnums and Long Rifle models) using Q-Tips. Please understand, if I were cleaning a match .22 rifle then I might well use another protocol. However, for my purposes (the practical use and maintenance of my handguns) I have found that Q-Tips serve my purposes very well.

I first dip a Q-Tip into my solvent. Then, depending on the length of my barrel, I either just run the Q-Tip through the bore or place the Q-Tip inside the bore and, using a thin wooden rod, push it through to the end. I do this several times.

Once that is done I run dry Q-Tips through the bore, then put some oil or Break-Free CLP on the end of one and push that through my handgun's bore a few times.

I've used this technique for quite a long time and the bores of my .22s look like mirrors.

*

Magazine Maintenance

Each pistol magazine will have a different method of disassembly. Your goal with your magazines is NOT to lubricate them, just to keep them free of dirt and debris as well as dry inside.

Some shooters keep two stocks of magazines; those for range use only and those set aside for service use.

Before using a new magazine it would be prudent to fire a number of rounds through it to ensure reliable functioning. Furthermore, after extensive use a magazine's spring might well require replacing. In any event, I like to keep a good quantity of magazines on hand for any semi-automatic handgun I use regularly.

*

Firearm Specific Techniques

Glocks

Because this is such a popular handgun I've included some basic maintenance suggestions in the book specific to this pistol design.

First, prior to manipulating the Glock for maintenance, remove the pistol's magazine and check to ensure you have an empty chamber. Stick a finger in the chamber to be sure. Really. Any ammunition in the vicinity should now be taken elsewhere.

While pointing the muzzle in a safe direction pull the gun's trigger.

Pull the slide to the rear about 5mm. At the same time pull down on both sides of the exposed slide release. Now, permit the slide to move forward and off the weapon's frame. The gun should be in three main parts:

> Slide/barrel/recoil spring
> Frame
> Magazine

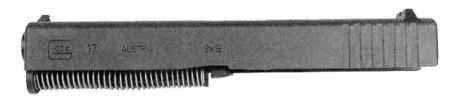

Glock 17 Slide Assembly

Glock 17 Frame and Magazine

Lubrication points

Glocks have three main parts, with from one to three lubrication points (more or less...) on each.

Slide

Lubricate (or grease, your call) the slide in three places: One small drop is placed on the slide's rails. Put a tiny amount of lubrication on the flat underside of the slide (and smear it around) and put an even smaller amount around the inside of the hole at the front of the slide which the barrel moves through. If you see white metal on the slide, that indicates metal to metal contact and that's a good place for a thin film of lubrication.

Barrel

Wherever you see indications of metal wear (white metal where there had been some coloration earlier), place a tiny bit of lubricant. Also, a tiny bit on the locking lugs under the barrel as well as on the top flat of the barrel where you see indications of rubbing metal.

Frame

One drop, inserted at the rear of the frame where there is a moving piece which is part of the trigger assembly should have a single drop of lubrication placed on it. With your Glock frame exposed move the trigger back and forth and you will see this part moving where the trigger bar connects to the connector. The area to be lubricated should be obvious at this point.

*

Other considerations:

> ➤ Firing pin channel must be clean and dry. No lubrication! Lubrication present in the channel will likely result in an eventual malfunction! (it collects debris)
> ➤ Recoil spring assembly should be clean and unlubricated.

> ➤ Don't put any lubrication in your magazines! Dry and clean is your goal here.

When reassembling your Glock ensure that the round plastic part of the recoil spring assembly end fits into the semi-circle piece on the underside of the barrel. If you install the recoil spring onto the ledge above this semi-circle you risk breaking off a bit of the plastic end-piece of this assembly. There are after-market recoil spring assemblies that use a stainless-steel piece in lieu of the plastic OEM design. I use such a unit in my Glock pistols.

With the slide/barrel and recoil spring in place, put the Glock's rails (at the front of the frame) into the slide's (rearmost) groves and pull the slide to the rear and back onto the frame. Work the slide a few times, pulling the trigger each time to ensure the firearm was put together correctly.

*

Reloading the Handgun

Once the firearm is cleaned and properly lubricated, unless there are exigent circumstances present, put the gun away for a period of time before loading it again. The reason I am urging you to do this is because, by the very nature and requirements of cleaning a handgun, you had to manipulate and handle the firearm in ways that were in violation of basic safety rules. During the cleaning process you undoubtedly pointed the handgun at various objects (perhaps even looked down its bore!) while you worked the action, pulled on the trigger and done other things to the firearm that you would not "normally" do. Your mind is in "gun cleaning" mode. If you immediately reload a firearm after manipulating it for cleaning there is the very real possibility that your unconscious mind will cause you to do something with the handgun (such as pull the trigger of a loaded weapon) that your rational mind knows is improper.

Give it a half hour or so before loading your handgun. Let your head catch up with your intentions.

When you do load your firearm, please ensure that the muzzle is pointed in a safe direction during the process. This is particularly important when reloading a semi-automatic handgun. There is a theoretical possibility (a very, very rare one) that when you permit the slide of your handgun to run home in order to put a round in the weapon's chamber the gun might accidentally discharge. Frankly, this most often happens when the "victim" of the accidental discharge has a finger on the trigger while performing this action. However, the stories that come after the "bang" rarely indicate that such was the case and "poor weapon design" often gets the blame.

For this reason, whenever possible I take my handgun/s outside when reloading my pistols. As I permit the slide to run home with a round in the magazine, I ensure my handgun is pointed at the ground. It's the prudent thing to do.

~

Handgun Suppressors

Quiet shooting! Sounds like an oxymoron. Until you've tried a suppressor –often referred to as "silencers"– on a handgun, you won't appreciate the pleasure of enjoying an afternoon's shooting, without the need to wear those annoying "ear-muff" sound barriers.

What exactly are suppressors? Well, what they are not what you've seen shown in the movies and on television; most often small cylinders stuck on the ends of assorted handguns (on occasion, even revolvers, a near impossibility), which turn powerful pistol shot sounds into little "poofs" of noise.

Nope, that's pure fiction. A suppressor simply slows down the speed of the expanding gases generated when a firearm is discharged. These devices work just like a car's muffler. Indeed, the inventor of suppressors, Hiram Percy Maxim (son of Hiram Stevens Maxim, inventor of the machine gun which carries his name), not only manufactured these devices for use with firearms at the start of the 20th Century, but made such devices for car mufflers as well!

This FREE Book
tells a lot about the
MAXIM SILENCER
Enjoy target shooting on your vacation with a single shot pistol or a rifle. It silences the report noise, lessens recoil, increases accuracy. Try one on your trip this summer and see how much more fun you have.
FOR FORD CARS we make a special Maxim Silencer. Applied to exhaust, it also saves gasoline.
Send for free book shown above full of interesting anecdotes of sportsmen. Ask your dealer to show you a Maxim Silencer; write us to send you the free book.
Maxim Silencer Co. 60 Huyshope Ave. Hartford, Conn.

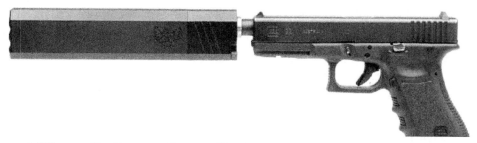

A SilencerCo Osprey 45 on a Glock 17. These are not small devices!

The theory behind how such pieces of equipment work is pretty simple. So long as the projectile is traveling at a subsonic speed, if the rapidly expanding gases generated by the firing of the gun are contained, slowed down to a sub-sonic speed, then the sound of the discharge is greatly reduced.

Having said that, I ought to point out that there are suppressors which have been designed, and are used, on high power rifles. This reduces the blast, muzzle flash, as well as noise of such firearms significantly. While they are still "loud," when compared to an unsuppressed rifle, such weapons are much, much quieter. In addition, when used in police and military applications, should such a weapon need to be fired indoors, its blast can damage the hearing of the firearm's user unless such a long arm is suppressed.

One word on the legality of suppressors. To lawfully possess a suppressor, you must comply with National Firearms Act (NFA) regulations. This law, put into effect in 1934, in order to "fight crime," lists suppressors as one of the items which the owner must first have a $200 dollar tax stamp from the government in order to possess. Mostly, the other types of firearms impacted by this law are:

> ➤ Short barrel rifles or shotguns
>   (with barrels shorter than 16" or 18" respectively),
> ➤ Fully automatic firearms,

Depending on the state you live in will determine whether or not you may possess one or more NFA classified items. If you may lawfully do so, according to your state's regulations, you first must comply with the federal requirements; filling out some forms and purchasing the $200 dollar tax stamp.

I do not wish to debate the logic of the NFA regulation in regard suppressors here, but I would like to state that, for all practical purposes, the law, in regard suppressors, is rather silly, for the following reasons:

> Some nations require citizens involved in the shooting sports to use suppressors, as this reduces the noise of the activity to the point where nearby citizens are not disturbed,

> A credible sound suppressor can easily be fabricated using a common oil or fuel filter. If a criminal were bent on committing some crime, would that person first take the time to lawfully purchase a suppressor, fill out the various forms, and then pay the $200 tax first??

I respectfully suggest that a more logical approach to suppressors would be to treat them as handguns are now handled. The purchase of the suppressor would entail the filling out of the federally mandated form 4473. State regulations would have to be followed for their possession and sale. One can hope.

HOW THIS WORKS

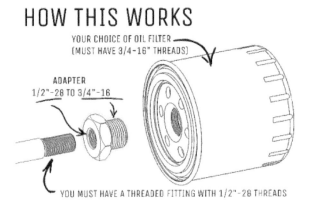

YOUR CHOICE OF OIL FILTER
(MUST HAVE 3/4-16" THREADS)

ADAPTER
1/2"-28 TO 3/4"-16

YOU MUST HAVE A THREADED FITTING WITH 1/2"-28 THREADS

No Tax Stamp = Very Illegal Oil Filter Suppressor

Legal Requirements

Forty-two (42) states in our nation permit possession of suppressors by their citizens. If you live in one of the following states, at the time this is written, your state does <u>NOT</u> permit you to purchase a suppressor:

California	Massachusetts
Delaware	New Jersey
Hawaii	New York
Illinois	Rhode Island

The basic information you need, in order to know if you may lawfully own a suppressor in one of the other states, is the following:

- ➢ Be a resident of the United States
- ➢ Be legally eligible to purchase a firearm
- ➢ Pass a BATFE[*] background check
- ➢ Be at least 21 years of age to purchase a suppressor from a dealer

[*]Bureau of Alcohol, Tobacco, Firearms and Explosives

You will be required to fill out a BATFE form 4 (the form applying for your $200 dollar tax stamp), as well as their form 5330.20 (which asks some basic questions about your immigration status). Don't let the paperwork put you off. Many dealers in suppressors will assist you in filling out these very short forms. The forms required are, to a certain extent, a "moving target," in that they can change. That's another good reason to use a reputable vendor when purchasing a suppressor (or any NFA item, for that matter).

I urge you to consider acquiring a "trust.". I think this is important if both you and your spouse are going to use the suppressor. A trust is a legal document which makes both parties lawful owners of the device. A number of suppressor manufacturers make creating a trust a relatively simple and inexpensive process, mostly by using "boiler plate" language in the trust forms they supply.

125

You will have to bring to the suppressor vendor a passport size photo of each person owning the suppressor (as when in a trust), you (and anyone else if you use a trust) will need to be fingerprinted (done at the store), and a money order, or certified check for $200 dollars, is also required for the tax stamp.

Suppressors in General

I think it simplest to discuss suppressors by breaking them down into two groups:

> Rimfire models, and,
> Center Fire models

Before I get into suppressors, I should first explain how the sound mitigated by these devices is measured. I'm not going to go into an overly technical discussion on the matter, which would likely put my readers to sleep.

Sound levels are measured by their decibel (dB) level. The manner this is done (and the noise level value assigned) is not intuitive. For each increase of 10 dB the sound is ten (10) times more powerful than the prior reference point. So, 70 dB is ten (10) times louder than 60 dB. If you double the dB reading, say from 60 dB to 120 dB, the noise power has increased by a million times!![1]

The threshold of pain, from noise, is around 130 dB. Most handgun suppressors reduce the dB level of their handguns, depending on caliber, from around 125 dB (center-fire handguns), down to approximately 115 dB (.22 long rifle firearms).

The rule of thumb is, sound levels beyond 120 dB, depending on length of exposure, can cause hearing damage, while the acceptable upper level impulse sound, according to OSHA is 140 dB.

Fortunately, firearms noises last only a fraction of a second, thus, when using a suppressed pistol, in general, hearing damage should not be an issue.

Richard P. Rosenthal

Rimfire Suppressors

Rim-fire suppressors are most commonly used with .22 long rifle, .22 Winchester Magnum and .17 Hornady Magnum Rimfire rounds. Because the intensity of the cartridges normally used in suppressors designed for rim-fire guns are of lower pressure, such suppressors are generally much lighter than their center-fire counterparts. Often the baffles used to slow down the expanding gases are made of aluminum, while the "guts" of center-fire models are most often made of steel or titanium.

Most rimfire types of suppressor are found threaded for use on 28x1/2" style threads. The "28" refers to the thread pitch, while the "1/2 inch" is the diameter. Which is good news, as center-fire versions come in many different and confusing sizes. There appears to be little standardization in the industry at this time in the center-fire field. So, yes, it can be perplexing to the buyer, once you're looking at other than rimfire suppressors. I'll discuss the issue in greater detail in the center-fire part of this chapter.

WWII .22 Caliber Military Suppressor

As mentioned earlier, there are three primary material inserts used for rim-fire suppressors; aluminum, titanium, or steel. There are important differences between them, which ought to be considered prior to purchase by the average user.

127

I own two .22 suppressors. Both are well made units, both are very quiet. One is a Surefire Ryder 22A, the other is a SilencerCo Sparrow. I like them both. However, the primary difference between the units is, one can be cleaned with a minimum of fuss, while the other is far more of a chore to remove the lead and powder build up.

It all has to do with the material the core of the suppressor is made of. My Ryder 22A baffles are aluminum, while the core of the Sparrow is made of stainless steel. With the Ryder unit, I have to remove the lead buildup mostly by hand, as I've yet to find any chemicals that will do the job to my satisfaction. My Sparrow, however, is amenable to the use of a combination of chemicals, referred to most commonly as "the dip," which removes the lead with no real work on my part.

A fifty/fifty mixture of White Vinegar and Hydrogen Peroxide (which combines to make peracetic acid) will remove the lead from suppressor baffles, HOWEVER, it will leave you with a toxic mixture of lead acetate. Lead acetate is toxic! You MUST wear protective gloves, as well as eye protection, should you opt to use this cleaning method. The container of this chemical must be disposed of as hazardous waste.

Here are additional warnings:

> ➢ Must use gloves when handling.
> ➢ Store in a glass jar with lid.
> ➢ Use in well ventilated space.
> ➢ Disposal must be done in proper manner! Each county should have a place to take your hazardous waste. Use it!

Understand this; you CANNOT use the dip for either aluminum or titanium baffles as the chemical will eat into either metal. I mean it, the dip will destroy both metals. The dip is ONLY for use with stainless steel baffles.

Another way to help keep your suppressor clean it so use rim-fire ammunition specifically designed for such shooting. I am aware of two manufacturers who, at this time, offer such loads in 22 long rifle ammunition:

- ➤ Federal 45 grain subsonic, copper plated lead round nose, and,
- ➤ Winchester, M22, 45 grain subsonic, black copper plated lead round nose

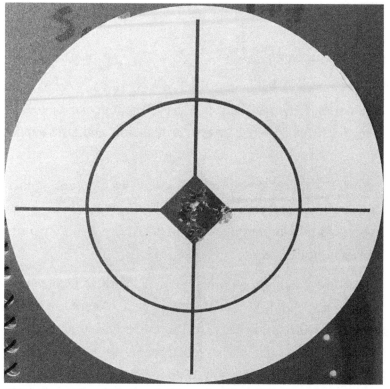

Five Rounds of Federal 45 grain Plated Subsonic, using a SilencerCo Sparrow Suppressor, Fired, From a Rest at 15 Yards. Pistol was a Ruger MK IV 22/45, with Vortex Venom Sight.

I own both rounds, but have mostly used the Federal ones. They have functioned reliably through my Ruger MK IV 22/45, and have proven very accurate. I have included in this chapter a sight-in target photo which demonstrates this.

I've found that, when firing "normal" lead .22 long rifle ammunition in my suppressors, the units become dirty very quickly. Indeed, if you permit too many rounds to go through your .22 suppressor, you may well find that the unit is locked shut, and requires a trip back to the manufacturer for opening and cleaning. Depending on company policy, that might prove expensive. I've found these plated rounds to be much, much cleaner, depositing far less lead in and among the suppressor innards.

Center Fire Suppressors

As this is a book about handguns, I will not go into any detail in regard rifle suppressors, although there is a certain amount of mutual utility (dependent on caliber) between certain handgun and rifle suppressor units.

Unlike rimfire suppressors, center-fire devices are not (generally) designed to be taken apart and cleaned. This is because there is virtually no exposed lead moving through the suppressor, thus eliminating lead fouling as an issue.

Most center-fire handgun suppressors will be used in one of three caliber handguns; 9mm, 40 S&W, or .45 ACP. There are numerous suppressors available for the user, so I'll only be discussing a very few here. As a practical matter, for anyone looking to buy a suppressor, it would be practical for that person to conduct a good deal of research prior to making a purchase.

A general rule of thumb to consider:

> ➤ A .45 caliber suppressor may be used with 9mm and .40 S&W handguns,
> ➤ A .40 S&W caliber suppressor can be used with 9mm handguns,
> ➤ A 9mm suppressor is suitable for, well, 9mm handguns, and,

> ➤ All of the above suppressors may be used with .22 rimfire caliber firearms, which I would not recommend!

First, why the no recommendation for the use of rimfire ammo being put through a center-fire suppressor? Because, you'll dirty up what may well be a difficult to clean suppressor, indeed, a model of suppressor that was not intended for servicing by the user at all. Center fire ammo is much "cleaner" than .22 rimfire ammo. Using .22 long rifle ammunition in a center-fire suppressor would simply be creating an unnecessary problem for yourself.

A Piston and Nielson Device Spring

Piston and Nielson Device

For a semi-automatic center-fire pistol, in those models in which the barrel tilts as the weapon cycles, in order for them to operate reliably, a special device must be affixed between the suppressor and the threaded end of a pistol's barrel. Basically, it's a spring buffer, along with a mating piece which matches your pistol's caliber, as well as the thread pattern of your pistol's barrel. This combination is referred to as a

Nielson Device (only one is required) and a Piston (which is different for each caliber).

If the handgun's barrel is "fixed." that is, the barrel does not tilt when the pistol is fired, there is another system used. A spacer is put on to the suppressor and the proper caliber Piston inserted. With such pistols, depending on model, there is either a fixed barrel spacer used, or the suppressor is specifically designed for that particular handgun.

Just a note; as far as I know, all .22 rimfire (.22 long rifle) pistols are fixed barrel types, and use neither a Piston nor Nielson Device, but are affixed directly to their suppressors.

Because there are so many variations among center-fire suppressor manufacturers I've created a section in which the various options are listed. Please don't let this be a cause of concern. Just make sure you've communicated with either the suppressor manufacturer, or the vendor you're buying the unit from, prior to making the purchase.

You'll need to know:

> What thread pattern should your barrel have for that brand of suppressor, and,
> Does the suppressor come with a Nielsen Device and Piston?

Many come with the Nielsen Device, which is generic, and at least one Piston suitable for the caliber you'll be shooting. Each different caliber requires a separate Piston, which are proprietary in design.

For example, when I purchased my SilencerCo Osprey 45, I also bought a threaded barrel from that company. Made my life much simpler!

I feel compelled to repeat my admonition:

Prior to purchasing a suppressor, speak to your vendor about the proper threaded barrel you will need (there are right, and left hand,

threaded suppressors out there!!), as well as the proper Piston, for your particular suppressor of choice!

Appropriate Ammunition

Rim-Fire

I've already discussed one way I've found to reduce lead fouling in my rim-fire suppressors, by use of copper plated, subsonic rounds. My experience with my rim-fire suppressors has been, conventional subsonic lead rim-fire rounds, while perfectly fine when fired in a non- suppressed pistol, can really "gunk up" the inners of a rim-fire suppressor.

One session trying to get the internal baffles of a rim-fire suppressor clean after using conventional lead subsonic rounds will convince you of the error of your ways!

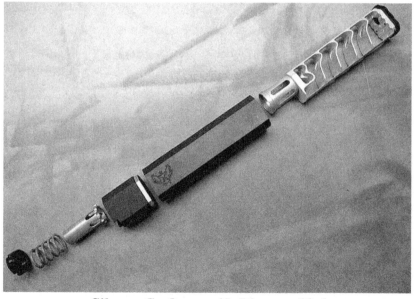

SilencerCo Osprey 45, Disassembled

Center-Fire

In order for a suppressor to be a "quiet" as it can be, the ammunition used when firing the pistol ought to be subsonic. Having said that, I've been around suppressed pistols when they were being fired with supersonic (9mm and .22 long rifle) ammunition, and the report wasn't bad, just not as quiet as when subsonic rounds were used.

With supersonic rounds, there is a distinctive "crack" as the projectile travels down range. I've found such ammunition to be considerably louder at the shooter's end as well. Not intolerable, just sort of defeating the purpose of the suppressor.

.45 ACP ammunition is, mostly, subsonic, particularly when firing 230 grain projectiles. 40 S&W, when using 180 grain rounds, is also subsonic. With 9mm, it's a bit more complex.

Projectile weights in 9mm (9X19mm, or 9mm Luger) range in weight from 115 grains up to around 147 grains (yes, there are exceptions). Generally, 147 grain rounds are subsonic, and are the preferred choice in that caliber handgun. The advantage of using 147 grain rounds is, these are full power loads, thus their less than supersonic velocities permit their use in suppressors without sacrificing any utility such round offer.

On Left: The First Three Baffles from my Ryder 22A Suppressor
~After a Cleaning~

On Right: A Lead Caked Aluminum Suppressor Baffle

Below are listed some suppressors, and their noise levels, in decibels (dB) which they generate. In the reference section you may find the document I've taken this information from, with data on 332 suppressors shown. For clarity I have rounded off some dB numbers in my table: [2]

Maker/Model	Caliber	Bullet Weight	Sound Level Without/With Supp.
AAC Aviator 2	.22 long rifle	40 grain	154.2/118 dB
Griffin Armament Checkmate QD	.22 long rifle	40 grain	154.1/120 dB
Surefire Ryder 9Ti	9mm	147 grain	159.3/133 dB
Osprey 45	9mm	147 grain	156.8 dB/125 dB
Osprey 45	.45 ACP	230 grain	161.4/133 dB

I've also included, below, some information on how loud long arms are, and how their sound levels are reduced when suppressors are utilized. Clearly, routine firing of center-fire caliber long arms, even when suppressed, will damage a person's hearing:[3]

Maker/Model	Caliber	Bullet Weight	Sound Level Without/With Supp.
AAC M4-2000	5.56mm	55 grain	168/140 dB
AAC SR7	7.62x51mm	147 grain	170/145 dB
Liberty Victory Magnum	7.62x51mm	168 grain	166.4/137 dB
SilencerCo Harvester Big Bore	7.62x51mm	147 grain	168/134 dB

Firearm Barrel Thread Patterns Most Commonly Encountered[4]

Here are some abbreviations used in the listed thread patterns:

➤ M=Metric (M13.5X1 LH, means these numbers are metric instead of standard)
➤ LH=Left Hand (M13.5X1 LH, means the thread pattern is backwards and threads on the opposite direction)
➤ RH=Right Hand (M16X1 RH, means the thread pattern should be the same as normally expected)
➤ TPI=Threads Per Inch

.22LR .22MAG, .17HMR:

1/2×28 is typically the standard thread size for those calibers. As such pistols are virtually all fixed-barrel, neither Nielsen Device, nor Piston, are required.

9mm:

1/2×28 is typically the most common thread for 9mm weapons, with the following exceptions:

➤ H&K: M13.5×1 LH
➤ Sig Sauer (MPX): M13.5×1 LH
➤ Glock: M13.5×1 LH
➤ Factory H&K MP5-N: 1/2-30

.40 S&W:

9/16×24 is typically the most common thread for .40 S&W weapons with the following exceptions:

➤ H&K: M14.5×1 LH
➤ Sig Sauer: M13.5×1 LH
➤ Glock: M14.5×1 LH

.45 ACP:

.578×28 is the most common thread for .45 ACP weapons with the following exceptions:

> ➢ H&K: M14.5×1 LH
> ➢ H&KUSP Tactical: M16x1 LH
> ➢ H&K Mark 23 (Socom): M16x1 RH
> ➢ Glock: M16x1 LH
> ➢ KRISS Vector SMG: M16x1 LH
> ➢ Sig Sauer P220: .578"-28

.223/5.56 NATO:

1/2×28 is the most common tread pattern for most AR-15s. However, there are some exceptions:

> ➢ Steyr Aug: M13x1 LH
> ➢ H&K: M15x1
> ➢ Ruger Mini: 9/16×24

.308/7.62mm:

5/8×24 is the most common tread pattern. However, there are some exceptions:

> ➢ SakoTRG: M18x1
> ➢ Accuracy International: M18x1.5
> ➢ AK-47: M14x1 LH
> ➢ FN SCAR 17: 5/8×24
> ➢ Springfield M1A SOCOM 16: .595×32

.338 Lapua Magnum:

5/8×24 is the most common thread pattern. However, there are some exceptions:

- ➢ SakoTRG: M18x1
- ➢ Accuracy International: M18x1.5
- ➢ Desert Tactical Arms: 3/4×24
- ➢ Barrett MRAD: 3/4×24
- ➢ Nemo Omen (.300 Win Mag): 5/8×24

.50 BMG:

- ➢ McMillian TAC-50: 1" x 14 TPI
- ➢ Armalite AR50: 1" x 14 TPI
- ➢ Barrett: 7/8" x 14 TPI
- ➢ EDM: 7/8" x 14 TPI

Richard P. Rosenthal

References Suppressors

[1]*North Carolina Silencer*:

http://ncsilencer.blogspot.com/2011/02/sounds-decibels-and-suppressors.html

[2]*ModernRifleman*:

https://modernrifleman.net/suppressors/

[3]ibid.

[4]*Modern Warriors*:

https://modernwarriors.com/common-barrel-thread-patterns/

Basic Discussion of Firearms and Ammunition

As is implied by the title of this book, Practical Handgun Training, I'm not going to take my readers too deeply into the history of firearms, ammunition, nor how the technology has evolved over the centuries. My fundamental goal is for the reader to have a comfortable familiarity with some basic information a person around firearms ought to possess. This is particularly so in regard caliber designations, the complexities of which seem to befuddle many.

I'm going to start the chapter at the beginning of the introduction of self- contained cartridges, thereby ignoring the thousand years of development that came before this period. If you took the time to read up on the ideas and inventions that have risen over the centuries in the field of firearms evolution, you'd soon see that many "modern" designs would have existed much earlier but for the lack of technical knowledge and material availability which existed during the period when they were first thought of. Think of Da Vinci and his ideas on man-carrying aircraft. Among other problems Da Vinci had was the dilemma of not having a suitable power plant available to operate his machines, an omission that would not be rectified until many centuries after he was gone.

While I personally find this subject an interesting one, I understand that many would rather involve themselves in other matters. So, I'll leave you with the thought that there are hundreds of fine books available on this topic for the reader to avail themselves of, should they desire pursuing the subject in greater depth.

Richard P. Rosenthal

Ammunition

First, some definitions. An unfired round is properly called a cartridge (not a "bullet"). It consists of;

> The cartridge case
> One or more projectiles, pellets or bullets
> Propellant, most often referred to as "gun powder"
> A primer needed to ignite the propellant

The first practical firearms cartridges, the type which eventually evolved into the rounds we are familiar with now, were developed around 1860. These were rimfire rounds (their priming compound being located in their soft rims) and were first seen in a .22 caliber revolver manufactured by the Smith &Wesson company (the .22 short, in 1857). A few years later came the .44 Henry rifle round (Henry being the name of the man who designed both the rifle as well as the cartridge) for the 1860 Henry rifle, manufactured by the New Haven Arms Company, which soon evolved into the Winchester Firearms Company.

Because rimfire type cartridges were limited in the amount of power they offered (their rims having to be sufficiently soft so that a gun's firing pin could dent it in order to ignite the priming compound contained therein), a stronger, more robust cartridge case was developed. Soon after came the development of the next system to be used; center-fire cartridges. These had the somewhat weaker primer part of the round (the part containing the priming compound, and which was designed to be struck by the firearm's firing pin or hammer) located in the center rear part of their much heavier brass (the most common material used) cartridge cases.

Two types of center-fire designs evolved; the Berdan type and the Boxer versions. Although the Berdan design was invented by an American (Hiram Berdan), this system ultimately become more popular in Europe. The Boxer design, while developed initially in Europe (by Edward M.

141

Boxer, of the Royal Arsenal, Woolwich, England), became far more popular in the United States!

The reasons for the switch, in short, was that while cartridges using the Berdan system are somewhat less complex (and less expensive) to manufacturer initially, its design made reloading the perfectly reusable (and relatively expensive) cartridge cases more difficult than with the Boxer system.

Cartridge Nomenclature

Cartridge nomenclature, as well as ammunition names, are confusing and difficult to understand. For example, when you are engaged in conversation with a person and they state, "My handgun is a 9mm," the individual could mean the cartridge the handgun is chambered for is the 9x17mm, a round also referred to as the 9mm Short, Corto, or by several other names. Or, perhaps for some other 9mm pistol cartridge, such as the 9mm Largo, Steyr, Glisenti or around a dozen other variants.

All of the above rounds are designated as 9mm cartridges, all have the same projectile diameter. Yet, each uses a different casing and cannot be used safely in a firearm chambered for another 9mm round. Those with the dual number designation (9x19mm is an example) simply indicate that the projectile diameter is 9mm and the length of the cartridge case is 19mm. The Europeans tend to use this simple and easily understood system.

Cartridges developed for early Colt pistols (semi-autos) carried the designation Automatic Colt Pistol, abbreviated ACP. These include the; .25 ACP, .32 ACP, .380 ACP, .38 ACP, and .45 ACP.

I don't wish to wander off into rifle cartridge designations but would like to at least mention that black powder rounds often were designated by caliber, the weight of black powder they were loaded with, and the weight of the cartridge's projectile. One common round so described is the early United States military round, the 45-70-405. Thus, we're speaking of a .45 caliber projectile, with 70 grains of black powder in the cartridge case, which fired a 405 grain bullet.

*

As mentioned earlier, an unfired cartridge is composed of several components; a casing, a projectile, a primer and propellant ("gun powder"). The basic information on ammunition follows.

*

Projectiles and Caliber

The weight of projectiles is measured in grains. There are 437½ grains in an avoirdupois ounce (7,000 grains to the pound). For example, here are some popular handgun projectile weights in both grains and in their (approximate) ounce weight equivalents;

Grains	Ounces
100	.208
124	.258
158	.329
230	.479
255	.531

So, from the above you can see that a 100 grain bullet weighs in at just over 2/10th of an ounce. A 230 grain bullet is nearly ½ ounce in weight. Most popular cartridges are commercially available in bullets of varying weights. Some common examples are, by bullet weight in grains (keep in mind that this list is not at all inclusive.

Extremes in bullet weights may be found for many commercially available rounds.):

Projectile Weights in Grains

.22 long rifle	33 ~	60
9x19mm	100 ~	147
.38 Special	110 ~	200
.357 Magnum	110 ~	170
.40 S&W	135 ~	180
.44 Special	200 ~	246
.45 ACP	185 ~	230

Projectile velocities are measured in "feet per second." This is abbreviated fps. As a reference, the speed of sound is approximately 1,100fps.

Handgun rounds are most commonly found made from lead, often with some jacket material surrounding the lead core. This is needed for the reliable operation of semi-auto pistols, as well as to prevent leading of the barrels of revolvers when higher velocity rounds are utilized. Such rounds are also useful as a way to reduce airborne lead contamination at indoor ranges.

For handgun use there are a number of common projectile shapes and configurations in common usage. These include:

Lead Projectiles:

- ➢ Round nose
- ➢ Wadcutter (a pure cylinder shape)
- ➢ Semi-wadcutter

144

Jacketed Rounds:

- ➢ Full-metal jacket ~ commonly used in the military and for training purposes
- ➢ Soft nose (lead exposed at the nose)
- ➢ Hollow-point
- ➢ Total Metal Jacket (TMJ) ~ used to reduce lead in the air at indoor ranges.

There are many, many variations in bullet structure, material and configuration. As a practical matter, a cartridge/projectile combination should be chosen based first on its reliable functioning in the handgun and, second, its accuracy in the firearm it is intended to be used in. Once those two factors are dealt with other criteria, depending on the use the firearm is to be put, may be addressed (to be discussed in more detail in the chapter on "Bullet Potential").

Generally, a cartridge is nominally designated by the diameter of its projectile (or bullet). But, not always. Some United States cartridge designations do not correlate to the actual diameter of the rounds that carry their names. For example, the .38 Winchester Center Fire (.38 WCF or .38-40) has a projectile diameter of .401 inch. The .44 WCF (.44-40) has an actual bullet diameter of .429, as does the .44 Special and .44 Magnum rounds.

Other examples of this off-putting system of cartridge designations are;

- ➢ .38 Special and .357 Magnum both use .357 diameter projectiles.
- ➢ .38 Smith and Wesson (also .38 Colt New Police) fires a .359 diameter projectile.

As I mentioned earlier in the chapter the Europeans frequently use a somewhat more rational system for the identification of ammunition. This consists mainly of the projectile diameter in millimeters plus, most often, by the case length in millimeters. Common handgun rounds using this system are the 9x17mm (.380ACP), 9x18mm (Makarov) and 9x19mm (9mm Luger).

Some older European handgun rounds utilize the projectile diameter plus a proprietary name. Examples are;

7.62mm Nagant	7.65mm Borchardt
7.62mm Tokarev	7.65mm Parabellum
7.63mm Mauser	7.65mm Mannlicher

None of the above cartridges, with the exception of the 7.62mm Tokarev and 7.63mm Mauser (which are, for all practical purposes, dimensionally the same round) are interchangeable.

The Europeans also frequently identify if the round is rimmed, adding the letter "R" in the designation to so indicate.

Sometimes rounds carry both a European and United States designations. Some common handgun rounds that fall into this category are the .32 ACP (7.65mm Auto, 7.65mm Browning) and the 9mm Luger (9x19mm).

Cartridge Cases:

Most often, modern cartridge cases (the part of the round which holds the propellant, bullet and primer as a single unit) are made of brass. Some aluminum cases are also on the market. Cases have, in the past, also been made of paper, plastic, various metal foils as well as of (soft) steel, which remains a popular cartridge case material in some Eastern European countries.

The cartridge case serves not only to hold every part needed for discharging the gun in a single unit, it also serves to protect the components of the round from contamination as well as to contain the high pressures generated when the gun is discharged (this is called obduration).

There are a number of variations in cartridge case types;

> Straight walled (.22 long rifle, .38 Special, .44 Special, .45 ACP)
> Necked (7.63 Mauser, .357 SIG)
> Belted (rifle ammunition only)

And, within those types, are different rim configurations, with some examples of each below;

> Rimmed (.32 Long, .38 Special, .44 Special, .45 Long Colt)
> Rimless (9x19mm, .40 S&W, .45 ACP)
> Semi-rimmed (.25 ACP, .32 ACP, .38 Super)
> Rebated rim (rim is of smaller diameter than the cartridge case. Except for some exotic handgun rounds, mostly found in rifles.)

For the handgun user, for all practical purposes, you should at least be aware of the existence of rimmed, rimless and semi-rimmed type cases.

Some ammunition designations defy logic or classification, so I'll simply point out a few of the more common ones you might run into, along with a bit of information on each, as well as the year the round was introduced. Understand, even among these rounds there are variations I haven't mentioned here;

45-70	.45" diameter projectile with 70 grains of black powder. Our first really successful self-contained military cartridge (1873).
38-40	.40" diameter round with 40 grains of black powder (1874).
44-40	.429" diameter projectile with 40 grains of black powder (1873)
30-30	.30" diameter round with 30 grains of **smokeless** powder. This was the first commercially available

smokeless powder round and the company used the old black powder system of nomenclature when it was introduced. (1895)

.38 Special	.357" diameter projectile (1898).
.357 Magnum	.357" diameter projectile (1934).
9x19mm	9mm or .356" diameter projectile with a case length of 19mm (1900).
.38 ACP	An obsolete –it came out in 1900– semi-auto pistol cartridge.
.38 Super Automatic	An older (1929) high-intensity round, which remains popular. Both the .38 Colt Automatic round and the .38 Super round share the identical cartridge case. Due to the higher pressure of the Super version *they are not interchangeable!*

An interesting fact is the date when many of the popular rounds in current use were first introduced. Here is a list of some cartridges and their dates of introduction;

.25 ACP	1905
.32 ACP	1899
.380 ACP	1908
9mm Luger	1900
.38 Special	1898
.357 Magnum	1934
.44 Magnum	1955
.45ACP	1904

*

Richard P. Rosenthal

Propellant

Although routinely referred to as "gun powder," both black powder and smokeless powder, so-called, are actually granulations of various sizes made from their respective materials. For the sake of convenience, I'll continue to refer to both as "powders."

Black powder is a mechanical mixture of saltpeter, charcoal and sulfur, and its basic composition has been around for about 1,000 years. The burn rate of black powder is a function of the size of the grains, although, since it's a low-grade explosive, there is more latitude in the amount of powder in a shell than is the case with smokeless powders, a propellant capable of much higher pressures.

Smokeless powder consists of granules of nitrocellulose, sometimes mixed with nitroglycerin (referred to as double-base powder). During the latter part of the 19th and early 20th century cellulose movie film was sometimes cut up by people living in more primitive societies and used as a propellant in discarded rifle cases (often British .303 rifle rounds). Strike-anywhere match heads served for priming. Not a procedure to be recommend, but it worked.

For smokeless powder, the rate of burn is largely dependent on the size and shape of the individual granules. Thus, while all smokeless powder material is, fundamentally, made of cellulose (there are variations due to chemicals added to the mix), fast burning pistol powder may have grains roughly the size of the period at the end of this sentence while a battleship's 16" canon (it threw a projectile weighing over a ton!) used a heavy powder charge the individual "grains" of which were the size of the human thumb. After World War II tons of surplus artillery powders were sold on the commercial market and reconstituted into suitably sized grains for use in conventional sporting firearms.

The vast majority of cartridges in use today use modern smokeless powders. There are even variants of smokeless powder used as a replacement for black powder, and may be substituted for black powder in a 1:1 ratio. This material is a more efficient propellant then black powder as well as safer to handle, albeit less sensitive to ignition, generally requiring modern primers be used when this type of propellant is employed.

Primers and Priming:

Primers are used to ignite the powder inside cartridges. There are two main types of priming systems in use today; center fire and rimfire. The rimfire system was first introduced as a practical cartridge ignition system in 1857 by Smith & Wesson. As the name implies, the priming compound is located spread around the inside of their soft rims. The .22 short round was the cartridge which was chambered in the first practical cartridge revolver of the period. Cartridge projectile diameters, as well as the power needed for them to be of practical use, increased rapidly, and, in 1860, Oliver Winchester introduced the Henry repeating rifle, firing a .44 rimfire round of the same name, a long arm which proved effective for both military and civilian purposes (this round is roughly comparable to the .45 ACP handgun in power).

Due to the need for more powerful rounds, and some inherent weaknesses on the part of rim fire ammunition, center fire rounds soon followed. The Colt Peacemaker of 1873 is an early handgun chambered for a center fire round, the .45 Long Colt.

For purposes of personal defense, the center fire priming system is the most common type found in use today. This is due to the greater power (and pressures) required of center fire rounds as well as the center fire cartridge's reputation for being the more reliable ignition source.

Until very recently the material in firearms primers had a significant amount of lead in it (lead styphnate). Due to concerns over airborne lead contamination, quite a few modern center fire cartridges are now manufactured without having lead as a component of the ignition charge. Such a designation would normally be visible on the box of ammunition the rounds come, in and would prove useful for indoor firearms practice.

*

Some common firearms and ammunition myths:

- ➤ The "One-Shot Stop," or, a single round will stop a determined assailant
- ➤ Shotguns never miss, nor do they need to be aimed
- ➤ Cars blow up after being hit by a firearm's projectile
- ➤ Hip shooting is faster than aimed fire

The "One-Shot Stop" Fantasy

I discuss this matter more fully in the chapter titled Bullet Potential. There seems to be a visceral need on the part of some folks to believe that a relatively low-powered weapon –the handgun– is capable of routinely stopping the actions of a determined armed adversary virtually every time the weapon is employed.

Because I go into this matter in some detail in the next chapter, I'll simply end this short discussion on the subject with a single thought. In World War II the United States military put in the field a delightfully light long-arm, the M1 carbine (and its variants).

This little rifle used a .30 caliber round which was reviled for its lack of "stopping power" as much as the small rifle was lauded for its utility due to its ease of carrying. The cartridge had the following ballistics:

.30" diameter / 110 grain projectile @ 1975 fps muzzle velocity

Yet, a popular, indeed, an excellent personal defense cartridge, the .357 Sig round, is considered by many to be one of the most effective personal defense cartridges currently available. Much is made of this round's ability to cause anyone struck by it to instantly stop their aggressive actions. The ballistics of the .357 Sig may be seen below:

.355" diameter / 125 grain projectile @ 1425 fps muzzle velocity

So, we are to understand that a handgun cartridge whose projectile is .055" larger in diameter than that of the .30 caliber carbine round, firing a bullet that weighs 15 grains more (recall, there are 437½ grains to the ounce), yet with 400 fps less velocity, is a formidable anti-personnel round?

Yes, I am aware that the .357 Sig is able to use expanding projectiles while the military was limited to fully jacketed projectiles for use in the carbine. And that does make a difference. None the less, I find the comparison between the two rounds, in light of the anecdotal stories about both which I've been told, and which I've read, to be worthy of critical reflection.

*

Shotguns can't miss and they blow things up!

How many times have you seen in movies and on television, when a shotgun is fired, the following takes place?:

➢ While being fired from the hip, a single shotgun blast not only strikes the intended target, but throws the person struck backward, quite often through a plate glass window.
➢ A shotgun blast aimed at an auto causes the auto's trunk to pop open and the car to burst into flames.

Once again, we are dealing with nonsensical fantasy. First, what exactly is a shotgun? Generally, it's a smooth bore (non-rifled) long arm designed to fire from one to many hundreds of pellets. A single pellet or projectile can weigh from just under to a bit over an ounce. Velocity of a slug is around 1,600 fps. It's a formidable round, effective both against game animals and human adversaries, particularly at close range. Yet, it cannot knock people off their feet. For every action there is an equal and opposite reaction. If the impact from a fired shotgun could knock a person down, then the shooter would also be knocked down.

A popular shotgun load for anti-personnel use is "00" buckshot. In a 12 gauge shotgun a magnum load of 00 buckshot consists of twelve pellets, each around .33" in diameter, each pellet weighing around 55 grains (the .25 ACP uses a 50 grain projectile or a bit over $1/10^{th}$ of an ounce), with a muzzle velocity of around 1,300 fps. This round, upon striking an adversary, will not cause that person to fall down. Furthermore, from a typical police issue shotgun barrel, such a round spreads its pellets out at about one inch for each yard beyond the shotgun's muzzle. So, at twenty feet from the muzzle the pellets would form a pattern of around **seven inches** in diameter. In order to have a chance at hitting your intended target you would have to at least have the front bead (or sight) of the shotgun pointed in the center of the target.

When training police officers in the use of the shotgun one exercise we had them go through was as follows:

The officers would ground their shotguns, already loaded with a single shell of 00 buckshot, twenty yards away from a combat silhouette target. They were instructed to pick up the firearms and hold them at port arms, finger off the trigger, round chambered, safety on. They were then directed to walk toward the targets and, on the command "hit 'em!," to fire at the targets from the hip.

The instructors would permit the student officers to get to within twenty feet of their individual targets before giving the command. Very, very few of the shotgun pellets ever struck any part of the silhouette targets. The point we made, and one you should understand is, if you intend to strike a target, even with a load of buckshot, you must use your sights! Hip shooting is, fundamentally, a waste of ammunition.

In regard the silly idea that a handful of dead-soft lead pellets would cause a motor vehicle to burst into flames is beyond ridiculous. While a shotgun blast at close range is a formidable anti-personnel weapon, the reality is, each individual pellet fired from a shotgun is of fairly low power. The largest diameter buckshot load is the 000 ("triple ought") round (eight pellets per shell is a typical 12 gauge load). Each pellet is about the same diameter as that of a 9mm or .38 Special bullet, about .36" in diameter, and weigh around 70 grains. Velocity at the muzzle is about 1,300 fps. Which would make each individual pellet somewhat more potent than a single .32 ACP pistol round (71 grain bullet at around 900 fps), which, I submit, is not a terribly effective round by any standard. A magazine full of .32 ACP rounds hitting a car would hardly cause the dramatic destruction of an automobile as is so often depicted in the entertainment media when displaying the consequences of a shotgun blast.

One final thought in regard the terminal effectiveness of a shotgun. There is no reason whatever that a load of buckshot striking an automobile would cause the car to burst into flames. All the pellets would do is break glass or put holes in the sheet metal. If they first strike a door there is little likelihood that the rounds will penetrate into the car's interior.

*

A final thought (and I am aware I'm drifting off-topic here). While there may be many, many hundreds of firearms calibers out there (and more seem to come out each year) don't become overly impressed when a "hot" new round comes along. The firearms industry seems to be forever on the lookout for some exciting new item to sell to the shooting public. Yet, for all practical purposes, a person would be suitably armed for life with long arms chambered in.22 long rifle and 30'06 caliber, along with them owning a 12 gauge shotgun. For handguns, while the problem as to which firearm to own becomes a bit more complex, it is not an insurmountable one. Depending on the task the sidearms are to be put you'd certainly want to possess at least one high quality .22 long rifle caliber handgun. If suited to your need and situation I'd suggest you acquire a sidearm designed for concealed carry. This would most likely be a good quality small frame .38 Special revolver or a compact semi-auto pistol chambered for a medium caliber round such as the 9x19mm or .40 S&W. A person would do well to own a service size sidearm, even if for use solely in home defense. Any caliber at or above the intensity level of the .38 Special or 9x19mm would do, really depending upon how much handgun recoil the individual can comfortably handle, and how accurately they can control the sidearm. For hunting "big game" a .44 Magnum revolver would be a great asset.

I've observed all too frequently in our affluent society that people try to "buy" skill and competency with gadgets and expensive equipment. The ability to safely and successfully handle a sidearm can only come with training and practice. An old saying went, "Beware the man who only owns a single gun, for he likely knows how to use it."

Probably as true a general maxim as was ever stated.

Shotgun Issues

While I am aware this book is primarily an instruction on the proper use of handguns, as this is a chapter discussing ammunition, I've opted to include a section on choke constriction and their impact on 00 buckshot loads.

During the Vietnam war the United States military experimented with assorted types of shotshells for use in jungle warfare. The testers found that two elements were important in reducing the spread of the shot, as well as increasing the lethality of shotshells to distances as far as sixty (60) yards downrange; the bores of the shotguns needed to be restricted from full choke to a somewhat smaller diameter opening and, the pellets need to be hard and actually round (you ever take a close look at a factory load of 00 buck?)!

As a practical matter, today most shooters will be limited to the quality of 00 and 000 buckshot loads which are commercially available. None the less, experimenting with shells manufactured by a number of different companies might prove useful.

When I was with the Firearms & Tactic Section I performed a simple test using two twelve gauge shotguns; a 20" barrel Ithaca model 37 with open choke and a sporting shotgun having a full or closed choke. I fired standard department issue 00 buckshot ammunition at distances from three (3) yards to twenty-five (25) yards. The photos on the following pages are the results of that test.

~

The photos on the following pages are side by side images of the results of firing an open choke versus a full choke shotgun, at various distances;

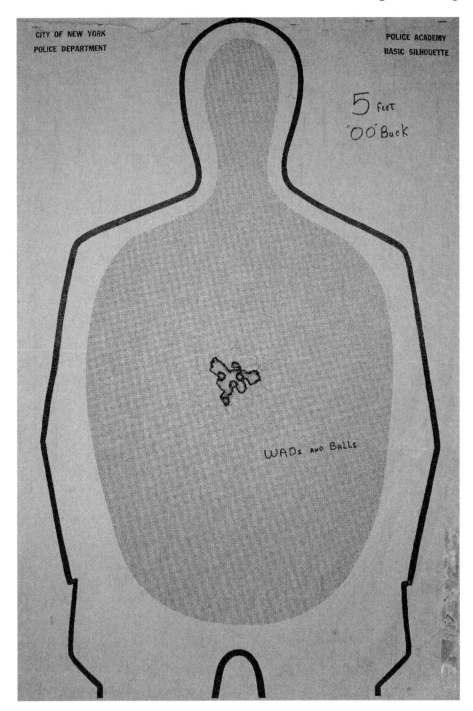

Open Choke 5 Feet

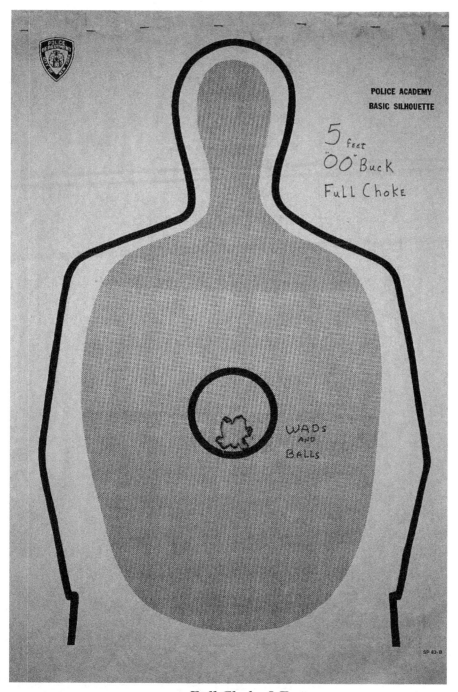

Full Choke 5 Feet

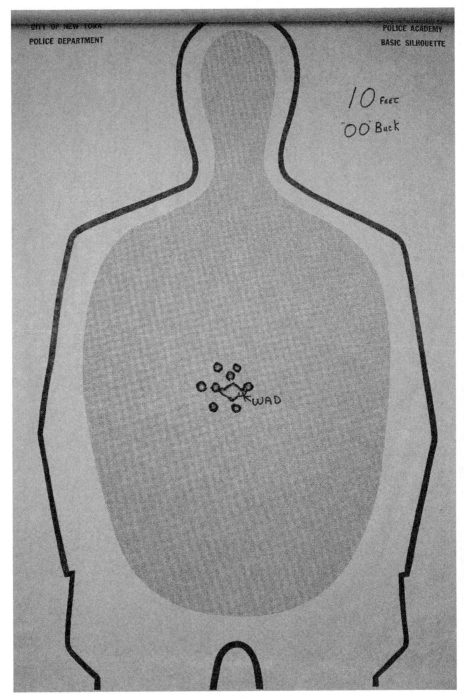

Open Choke 10 Feet

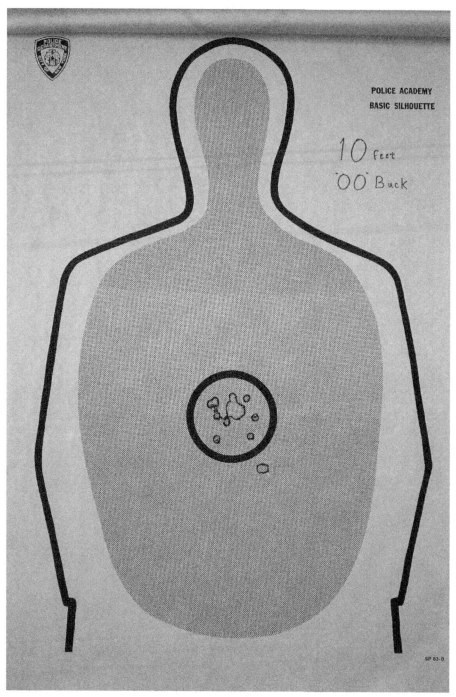

Full Choke 10 Feet

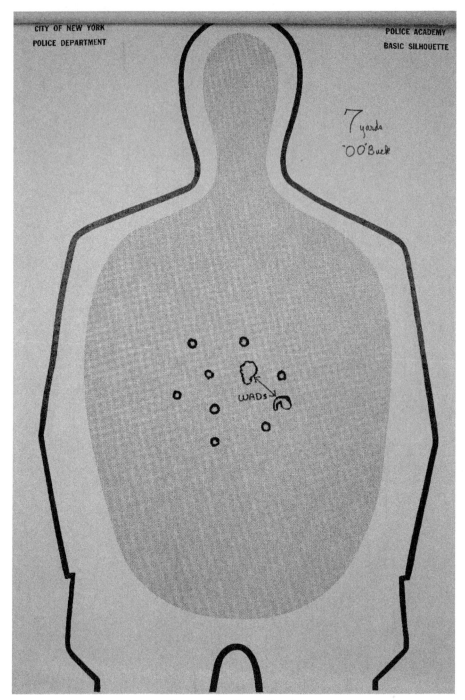

Open Choke 7 Yards

Richard P. Rosenthal

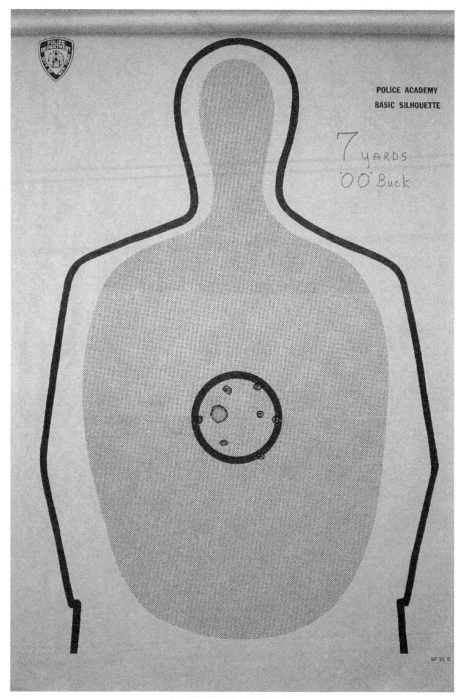

Full Choke 7 Yards

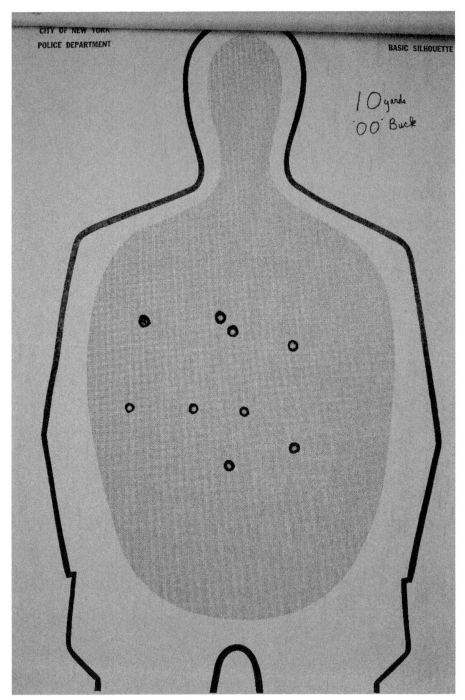

Open Choke 10 Yards

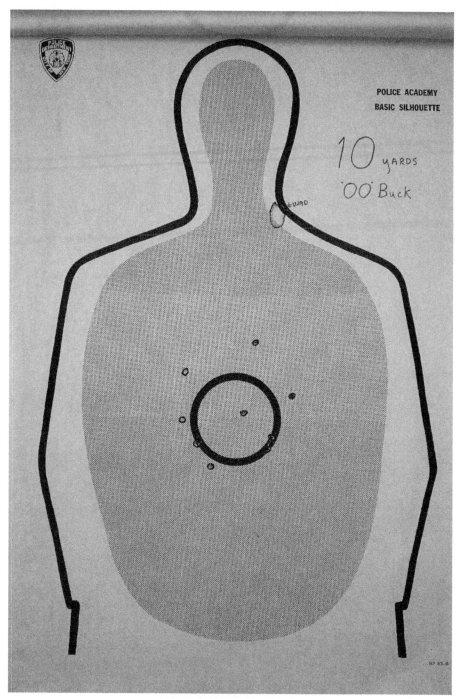

Full Choke 10 Yards

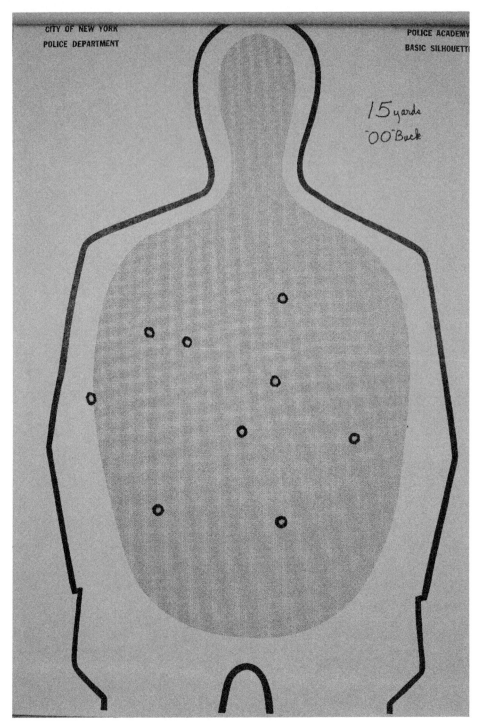

Open Choke 15 Yards

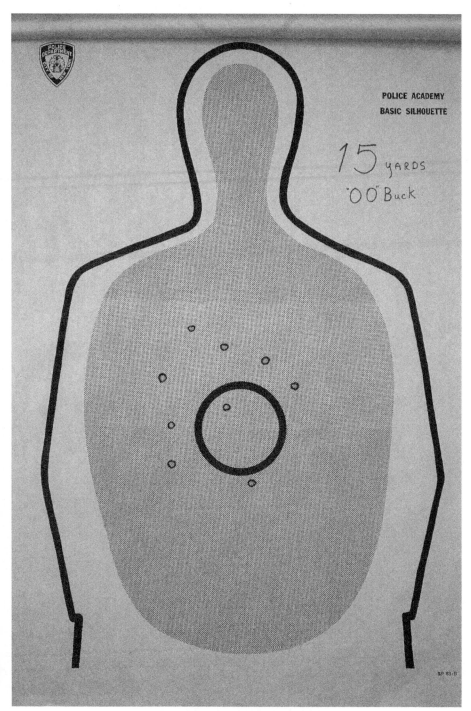

Full Choke 15 Yards

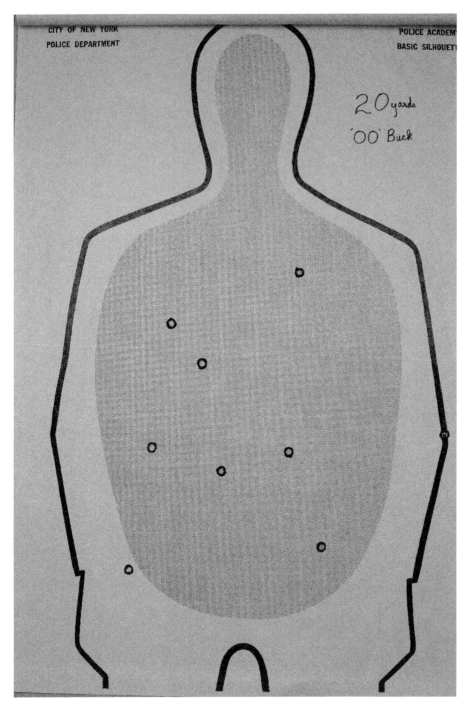

Open Choke 20 Yards

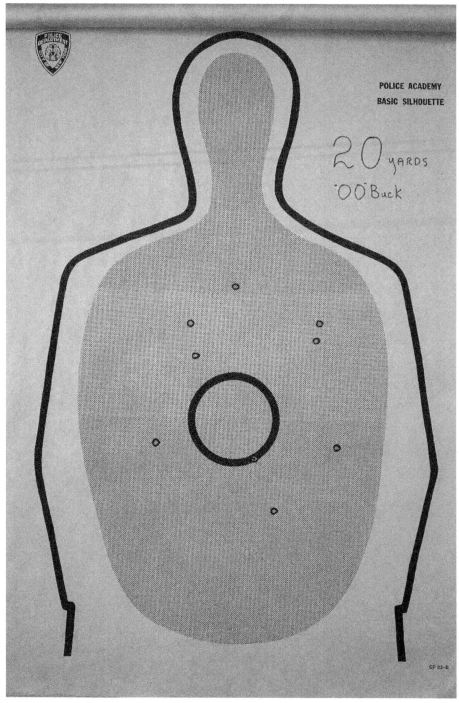

POLICE ACADEMY
BASIC SILHOUETTE

20 YARDS
'00' Buck

SP 83-B

Full Choke 20 Yards

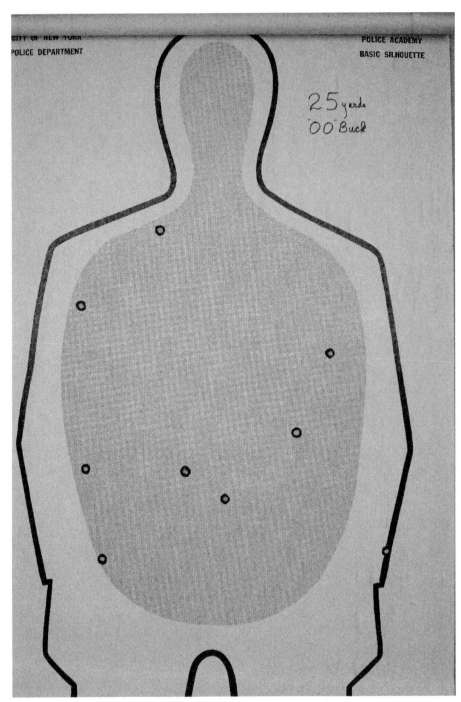

Open Choke 25 Yards

Richard P. Rosenthal

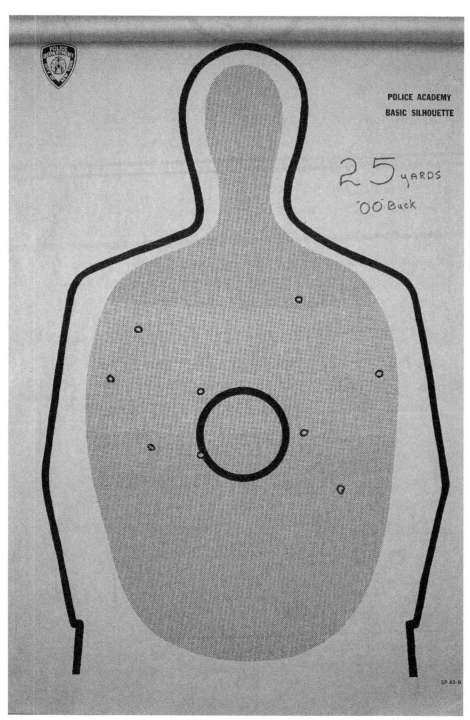

Full Choke 25 Yards

171

From these photos it should be clear that a constriction on the shotgun's bore has some impact on the effective range of 00 buckshot. I submit, if I were developing a shotgun for either military or law enforcement use, I would strive to achieve two goals:

> Develop shotshells with hard cast, truly round, not the dimpled pellets we most often see today, of either
> 00 (.33"/ 54 grains) or,
> 000 (.36" / 70 grains) size
> Find the correct bore diameter (choke size) for the issue shotshell in order to maximize the weapon's effective range

I am confident that with some experimentation a formidable anti- personnel shotgun round, capable of keeping its pellets within the center of mass of an adversary at ranges likely beyond forty (40) yards, can be developed.

From the photos it is clear that a shotgun, loaded with 00 buckshot, is not an "area" weapon. If the shooter intends to strike their target then at close range the front sight must be used and, as the distance from the target increases, then, at minimum, a rough, or flash, sight picture would be in order.

Indeed, with either an open or full choke shotgun, the photos show that at the most common combat distance, seven (7) yards, failure to utilize the shotgun's sights will likely result in a clean miss of the intended target.

Richard P. Rosenthal

Basic Discussion Firearms and Ammunition References

There are many fine sources of information out there in regard the history of firearms and ammunition. One source which I'm comfortable in recommending (and which I used during the writing of this chapter) is the <u>Cartridges of the World</u> series of reference books (currently in its 10th edition). This work not only covers every conceivable round ever invented, but explains in some detail the subtleties of cartridge nomenclature, and contains much information on gunpowder, primers and more.

Bullet Potential (Terminal Ballistics)

A Discussion on Choosing the Appropriate Handgun and its Ammunition

Executive Summary

It is not practical, based solely upon a handgun's caliber and cartridge combination, to accurately foretell what the end result would be when one person shoots another during a combat confrontation. Handguns simply lack the power, and humans are too unpredictable in their ability to absorb physical trauma, for such to be a real-world possibility.[1]

*

For some reason discussions on the subject of handgun projectile effectiveness frequently devolves into acrimonious debate. What should be reasoned discourse regarding the known facts revolving around the consequences of the combat use of the handgun too often seems to result in personal attacks being generated on the part of those participating in the discussion. I have no rational explanation for this, I am simply sharing an observation.

Therefore, I'd like to offer the following in regard my ability to know in advance the consequences of a gunfight, based solely on the cartridge/bullet combination used by the combatants. After forty years in law enforcement, including a stint as a New York City homicide detective, as well as a supervisory member of the NYPD Firearms and Tactics Section, I wish to point out that:

I have not a clue how a combat confrontation might reasonably be expected to end, based on the rounds used by either party. The only variables that I am aware of, and which a shooter has some control over, and which might otherwise influence the outcome of such an encounter, would be:

> ➤ The location where the projectile entered the person's body (determined, to a limited degree, by training and, to a far

greater degree, by the circumstances and situation in which the shooter finds him or herself in)

> The depth of the projectile's penetration into the body
> The width of the permanent cavity produced by that projectile

The variables over which there is no control over are:

> The mental state of those in the fight
> The chemicals in their bloodstream during the encounter

Those last two variables have a far greater impact on the outcome of a gun battle than all other aspects. Simply put, there are some individuals who will not quit. Even when mortally wounded, some people will fight on until they lose consciousness from loss of blood, or until their central nervous system is destroyed.

As to what chemicals are in a person's system at the time of a confrontation, these could be the result of a naturally occurring body reaction (the fight/flight stimulus) such as adrenaline, or chemicals taken through self-medication; alcohol, opiates, one of the many synthetics, or cocaine.

The consequences of a gunfight once begun, particularly when the weapons used are limited to handguns, is largely unknowable. Be cautious of anyone trying to convince you that a particular caliber/projectile combination has a "documented" ability to stop an adversary some specified percent of the time. Be most skeptical when that percentage of "one shot stops" is offered down to the tenths of a percent.

Indeed, it would be a physical impossibility for a firearm projectile, discharged from any hand-held weapon, to actually "knock a man down." The myth of a .45 caliber pistol round, upon striking a person in the thumb, which then knocks that person to the ground, is ridiculous and nonsensical.

The owner of a "bullet-proof" vest company, Second Chance, would routinely have himself shot, by an assortment of heavy caliber handguns (including the .44 Magnum) as well as .308 caliber rifle rounds, while wearing one of his products. Sometimes he'd be shot while standing on one foot. He never lost his balance or fell down, yet his body absorbed every bit of energy from the rounds which struck him.

I repeat. No firearm in normal use, when fired against another human being, has the ability to knock that person to the ground.

Having served in various functions within the NYPD, and, as stated earlier, the assignment most germane to this discussion having been that of homicide detective, I can accurately state that my empirical observations have been that once the gunfire starts there is no way to predetermine the outcome of the fight, nor how the participants will react upon being struck by gunfire. I have seen the result of bullets bouncing off people (after striking various parts of the body, including skulls), I have observed people survive and fight on after multiple hits with heavy caliber handguns, I have observed the outcome of what would have had to have been defined as a "one-shot stop" of a young large healthy male, with a single .25 ACP round to the small of his back. In point of fact, an experienced police firearms instructor told me of a one-shot stop that resulted from a blank going off, the victim of this prank having fallen to the ground, crying out he'd been hit!

I can explain none of them.

Later in my career within the NYPD, upon being assigned to the Firearms and Tactics Section, I used my position as head of Research and Testing to reach out to other police departments upon learning of various officer-involved shootings around the country.

I quickly discovered that news reports of these incidents were abysmally inaccurate. My second realization was, even the officers involved in these shootings sometimes had a hard time keeping the facts straight as to what had transpired during their incidents, a consequence, in my view, resulting from the officers preoccupation and focus on trying to remain alive at the time of the action.

Permit me to share with you my personal prejudices in regard the relative effectiveness of handgun projectiles. All else being equal;

For Non-Expanding Projectiles:

> The wider the projectile's diameter, the heavier the bullet's weight, the higher its velocity, the flatter the projectile's nose area (the wadcutter or cylindrical shape being the optimal configuration), the more effective the round will be.

For Expanding (Frangible) Projectiles:

> The wider, the heavier, the higher the projectile's velocity, assuming a bullet that will reliably expand, and still hold together, and which, even should the hollow of the round's nose fill with material from the target's outermost garment, continue to reliably expand, should prove to be the more effective round.

Long arms chambered for rifle calibers are another matter. Their anti-personnel dynamics, when they are used for personal defense, are beyond the parameters of this discussion. Simply put, any long arm, of deer rifle cartridge or greater power, should prove to be an effective anti-personnel round. Granddad's old lever action Winchester 94, in 30- 30 caliber, is a far superior anti-personnel weapon/cartridge combination then any practical-to-carry personal defense handgun now available.

Modern handgun ammunition has come a long way since I first became a police officer. I recall once, while visiting the ballistics lab up at the (now old) Police Academy on 20th Street in New York City, going through packets of rounds taken from the bodies of homicide victims (back then we averaged around 2,000 homicide victims a year in the city). At the time all the hollow nose rounds I observed had wads of cloth and bits of leather stuck in their hollows, effectively turning them into solid nose projectiles. I observed no expansion in any of them. My understanding is that modern projectiles do not suffer, to the same degree, the disabilities of those earlier designs.

I urge you to procure ammunition from a major manufacturer for your personal use for any handgun you've chosen for self-defense. Avoid exotic, niche rounds. Do not believe what you read in popular gun magazines (or see on the internet!) in regard handgun ammunition effectiveness. The sole reason these magazines exist is to sell advertising space. This is not an evil thing, but they are in business to make money. These magazines are not designed to relay data driven, independent and unbiased reports of fact.

Critically evaluate the recommendations of well-meaning friends in regard one handgun round's purported superiority over another. Ask yourself, how did this person come upon his or her knowledge?

Don't buy "magic bullets." We've already discussed the limitations of handgun effectiveness, and I assure you human physiology has not been altered to suite whatever brainstorm some bright-eyed inventor is currently hawking as the hottest round out there. Available at a premium price, of course.

Rounds that are composed of tiny pellets, held in jackets and pushed at relatively high velocity, tend to be shallow wounders. At several dollars a round, even if they were effective, how many could you afford to put through your personal defense pistol in order to ensure reliable functioning. Stay with proven designs.

The best way to determine which round ought to be carried would be to look at what larger law enforcement agencies are issuing their personnel. In large police agencies rounds that fail to either function reliably in their semi-automatic pistols, or which have poor reputations after evaluation of their use in the field, are soon removed from service.

I've found that the Federal Bureau of Investigations (FBI) study on handgun projectile effectiveness to be the most sophisticated work done on the subject by a law enforcement agency. The Bureau has significant resources at its disposal, with highly knowledgeable staff, has no desire to "sell" anyone anything, and is simply trying to evaluate ammunition based on data and reasoned observation of field confrontations. I am inclined to believe that, as they use this testing protocol to determine what ammunition is issued their agents, they've chosen to issue the most effective ammunition currently available based on their testing procedure.

This material is available to the public and is worth careful review.

Keep in mind that should you opt to carry some exotic round in your pistol, how many of these likely expensive cartridges will you be willing to put through your sidearm in order to establish their reliability in your particular handgun? I respectfully suggest that you should not carry any round that you have not successfully fired from your handgun, without malfunction, no less than a hundred times.

As an aside –and once again I ask your indulgence as I segue off-topic for a moment– revolvers are somewhat less sensitive to ammunition variations. None the less, it is prudent to fire any revolver at least a hundred times before first putting the gun into service. In this case, the bulk of the ammunition fired may be less expensive training rounds. I would still urge the firing of several dozen service rounds of whatever new personal defense ammunition you desire to carry in your revolver, certainly a sufficient number to determine where that handgun's point of impact is with that round as well as to ensure that the projectile doesn't "creep" forward from recoil and cause the handgun to malfunction.

Many years ago I acquired a brand new Colt Detective Special, purchased from the NYPD's Equipment Section. I dutifully took the handgun down to the Police Academy's indoor range (on 20th Street in

Manhattan) with the goal of firing one hundred rounds from the gun prior to carrying it. On the <u>very last cylinder full of ammunition</u> (target wadcutters), the cylinder locked closed and would not come open!

As I was at the range during normal working hours, I walked fifty feet over to the department pistolsmith at work there (Kenny Socker) and, fifteen minutes later, once again had a perfectly functioning revolver! My point being, you have to test fire any handgun prior to putting the sidearm into service for personal protection. I'm appalled by the number of people who walk into a gun store, buy a handgun and a box of ammunition, load the handgun, and proceed to carry the weapon, telling themselves they'll get to the range "someday soon."

Although this discussion is mostly about ammunition, I'd like to offer a word of caution in regard procuring semi-automatic pistols. Research your options carefully or you may end up purchasing a very expensive and frustrating "project." Only a short time ago, while at the site for firing my own qualification for the Law Enforcement Officers Safety Act, I was chatting with a fellow retired officer. He had a virtually new, very expensive, 1911A1 type pistol with him. It was not functioning reliably. He told me he had called the manufacturer and was told by them that the gun needed to have five hundred rounds fired through it for it to be "broken-in" before they'd even look at it for him!

No newly manufactured pistol should need to be "broken-in." Any handgun you purchase <u>should</u> work perfectly out of the box. You are not part of the company's quality control or research and testing department. You are a customer. Firearms are expensive. I am disheartened by the lack of quality routinely accepted by buyers of quite a few of the very expensive handguns being manufactured today that I am familiar with, as well as the general acceptance of the mantra that any newly purchased (generally when speaking of semi-auto) handguns "need to be broken-in" for them to be reliable. Nonsense.

180

Don't misunderstand. I am not suggesting that you should not first fire several boxes of ammunition from any newly acquired handgun which you intend to use for personal defense. That's only common sense as you're buying a machine, made by people, that could be defective. It's only that, when purchasing a new sidearm, I would expect the firearm, so long as good quality ammunition is used, to operate flawlessly during this validation and familiarization period.

Avoid purchasing a newly introduced handgun. Permit the bugs and weaknesses of the design to work themselves out at the expense of others. Read reviews of the handgun from those without a financial interest in the matter. Evaluate those reviews you do read or watch on video critically.

I'd like to offer up one last note on "stopping power." In 1848, while working as a foreman of a work gang blasting rock for a railroad's roadbed, twenty-five year old Phineas Gage was tamping an explosive charge of black powder into a hole when the charge went off. The four foot long, 1 ¼" diameter, 13 ¼ pound pointed bar he was using entered Gage's head below his left eye and exited the top of his skull, landing some distance away. Gage did not lose consciousness and required little assistance walking to his horse drawn buggy, in which he was taken to his rooming house about ¾ mile away.

Gage waited there for about an hour until a physician came. He was eventually helped to his bed, where he lay, semi-comatose, for a number of weeks. He eventually recovered and returned to leading a relatively normal life. Gage died in 1860.

So, the next time someone tries to regale you with tales of the relative effectiveness of one particular handgun's caliber or projectile type over another in its ability to "stop" an adversary, just remember the story of Phineas Gage.

Bullet Potential (Terminal Ballistics) References

[1]There are a number of theories as to the actual dynamics of how a firearm projectile causes cessation of activity with whichever creature it hits. A major debate exists as to whether hydrostatic (or hydraulic) shock is a controlling phenomenon in regard this concern. Knowledgeable people, including highly experience trauma physicians, cannot seem to agree on the matter. For further reading on the subject you might start with the Wikipedia section on Hydrostatic Shock:

http://en.wikipedia.org/wiki/Hydrostatic_shock

The citations offered there will permit you further research into the subject to the degree you desire.

[2]The incredible case of Phineas Gage, Neurophilosophy, December 4, 2006;

http://neurophilosophy.wordpress.com/2006/12/04/the-incredible-case-of-phineas-gage/

Practical Concealment of the Handgun

The title of this chapter states its goal; the information it contains is designed to be an overview on where and how to conceal the personal defense handgun, with a real-world look toward the practical limitations most people who wish to go about armed must deal with. In other words, what is the most *practical* and *task* related way to handle the problem.

Where one lives, the kind of work a person does, the culture of the people around them, all will impact the size of the handgun carried and how well it must be concealed. There are parts of the United States in which it is most unusual for a citizen to go about armed. Indeed, in New Jersey and New York City only but a very few law-abiding individuals are permitted to routinely travel about while lawfully carrying a concealed handgun. Thus, in that part of the county, most folks are totally dependent on an armed police force to protect them from threats of violence. Travel to Arizona, or some of the other south-western states, and you'd find there are citizens routinely moving about with firearms readily available for their use.

*

Firearm Size Options

The larger the handgun (when discussing concealed weapons, only handguns need apply) the easier for the user to hit their intended target, the larger (and more effective) the caliber a firearm may be chambered for, and the greater the number of rounds which may be carried in it. The problem lies in the fact that, generally, the larger and heavier the handgun the less easily is the sidearm concealed, as well as being less comfortable to carry. So, in order to be practical, we must accept a trade-off; whatever firearm we opt to keep on our person must be readily concealable, easily accessible, and able to be carried all day in comfort, all the while being reasonably effective as an anti-personnel weapon. To be successful will likely entail compromise.

A service size handgun (Glock model 23, Sig 220, Colt 1911, and its variants, are just some examples) will weigh in, loaded, at from about thirty to around forty ounces. This size handgun, with a few exceptions, is best worn in a strong-side, form fitting holster, attached to a specifically designed "combat" gunbelt. This type of gunbelt is made of two pieces of leather (a double thickness belt), with a width of from one and a quarter inches (1¼") to one and three quarter inches (1 ¾"). The outer portion of the belt must be stitched with nylon thread over the entire length of its edge for added rigidity and support.

Buying a good quality (read; custom) holster and attaching it to a dress belt is a waste of money as well as being counterproductive. A handgun worn in this manner will be flopping about all over the place. It will be uncomfortable to wear and to conceal, as well prove more difficult to remove from the holster when needed most.

Unless the handgun carrier lives in a situation where they can comfortably wear a secure holster (worn inside the waist band or outside the pants) along with a sturdy combat belt, both constructed for the specific task of aiding in the securing and concealing of a sidearm, the practical size of the handgun to be carried will be limited. As a general rule this will depend on how a person intends to carry their concealed handgun. If worn in the pants pocket such a weapon should best be between roughly ten (10) to fifteen (15) ounces in weight (Ruger LCP, S&W 342 = ±10~14 ounces, S&W 642, Ruger LCR, Ruger LC9 = ±15~20 ounces) As an experiment consider this, a can of soda weighs around fourteen (14) ounces. Toss one in your pocket for a day to get an idea of what carrying around a "lightweight" handgun feels like.

I am aware there are people out there who state that they comfortably wear a service size handgun on their person all day. More power to them. When I served as a detective in the NYPD, and while on duty, I routinely carried two handguns secured around my waist; a full-size S&W model 10 with four (4") inch heavy barrel (±40 ounces loaded) and a Colt Detective Special (±30 ounces loaded). With the additional six (6) round ammo pouch I had on my belt, plus a pair of handcuffs in a leather case, I toted about, on my person, sixty-five (65) or seventy (70) ounces of weight. No problem. My sport jacket covered the handguns and, frankly, I didn't really care if they showed.

That was then, this is now. My carry handguns currently weigh in at from ten (10) to seventeen (17) ounces empty (Ruger LCP in .380ACP, Ruger LC9 in 9mm Luger, S&W 342, S&W 642 and Ruger LCR, the last three in .38 Special caliber). And I do take care that no one around me notices that I'm armed.

Looking into my crystal ball I am confident in stating that if you purchase a handgun that is either too large, bulky or heavy for comfortable routine concealed carry, then, after a few frustrating times toting the gun around, that sidearm will be left home. And that will do you not one bit of good.

*

Calibers

All else being equal, the larger the caliber handgun the more effective it will be for personal protection. The heavier the weight of the projectile fired (when discussing ammunition designed for personal protection), the greater the firearm will recoil. My S&W 342, a .38 Special caliber, extremely lightweight (11 ounces unloaded) revolver, is a brutal handgun to fire. It's a fine pocket piece, an in-close personal protection handgun that gets fired perhaps ten rounds a year. This same weight handgun is available in .357 magnum caliber. The recoil of that round, in such a light weight handgun, could well damage the hands of some shooters.

Sticking with my self-imposed handgun weight limitations leaves, as a practical matter, five calibers to choose from:

> ➢ 380 ACP (also known as the 9x17mm and 9mm short)
> ➢ .38 Special
> ➢ 9mm Luger (9x19mm or 9mm Parabellum)
> ➢ .357 SIG
> ➢ .40 S&W

I've listed the calibers in order of theoretical effectiveness (I cannot say, as I do not know, which is the more effective round, the .357 SIG or the .40 S&W. Either one is a fine cartridge for their purpose.). Permit me some wiggle room here, as there are people who would also debate the .38 Special/9mm Luger bullet potential issue in regard which is the superior round. Flip a coin if you wish, in my view it's pretty close between them.

The .380 ACP is a fine pocket pistol caliber. I've fired many rounds in my diminutive Ruger LCP and, while not wildly fun, the recoil is more than tolerable. The debate with this round is whether to avail yourself of a modern expanding round or rather use a flat nose hard cast or fully jacketed projectile for self-defense.

Why is this an issue? This caliber is, in truth, very light for personal protection. As you've read in my chapter on bullet potential (you did read that chapter, didn't you?), there is a trade-off with handgun calibers between the ability of a projectile to expand, thereby increasing the width of the permanent cavity it creates in your adversary, versus the ability to penetrate deeply enough in your opponent to ensure effectiveness.

An expanding projectile in .380 caliber may or may not penetrate sufficiently into the torso of the person you are defending yourself against due to the "parachute" effect of the expanding round. The minimum penetration goal is around twelve inches (12") into the body. After such a round goes through the outermost garment of your assailant, and in consideration of the fact that there is an excellent possibility your antagonist may not be directly facing you (thereby likely putting his vital organs some further distance away from you), creates a potential issue when using expanding rounds.

I truly do not know the definitive answer to this conundrum. I carry a fully jacketed flat nose projectile round in my Ruger LCP.

*

Action Types

For our purposes we will limit this discussion to two handgun actions; the semi-automatic pistol and the double-action revolver.

Semi-auto pistols are:

> ➢ Flatter than revolvers
> ➢ Hold more ammunition than revolvers
> ➢ Require more training than with revolvers
> ➢ Tend to be less safe in the hands of the occasional firearms user than is the case with revolvers

Most people do not appreciate the difficult and life-threatening situation they put themselves in when procuring a sophisticated semi-auto handgun and not taking the necessary training to learn how to properly use, carry and handle their sidearm in a safe and effective manner.

What manipulations do you need to have down "cold" when carrying a semi-auto?

> ➢ Finger off the trigger until handgun is on target (this goes for revolvers as well!)
> ➢ Malfunction drills (several types) must be second nature (this requires much training)
> ➢ Safely clearing (unloading) the pistol must be fully mastered
> ➢ Safely loading the pistol must be mastered as well

The modern, double-action revolver has the advantage of being a simpler mechanism to learn and use. Generally, so long as there is good quality ammunition in the handgun's chambers, this type of sidearm will fire with each pull of the trigger, with virtually no chance of a malfunction that would tie the revolver up or otherwise put the gun out of action. Among this type of mechanism's advantages are:

> ➤ The handgun is always ready. No safety to forget. No springs under compression
> ➤ They are very reliable
> ➤ They are not ammunition sensitive
> ➤ The models with concealed hammers are very "pocketable"

Perhaps the most important advantage of the revolver is that they are the most practical, useful and suitable type of handgun for use as a personal protection tool for the occasional firearms user. Most people, police officers included, should be considered occasional firearms users.

This means, simply stated, that the amount of routine handling and firing of their sidearms they do is limited. Indeed, if police officers were not mandated to undergo supervised training on a regular basis, then issuing them semi-auto pistols would be irresponsible. Having known many law officers during my career, including significant numbers of retired members of various law enforcement agencies, I can assure you that the vast majority of these retired guys get out to a firing range but perhaps once every few years. Some, never.

Furthermore (and stated not in an effort to further antagonize my readers, honest!), the most suitable revolver for most individuals, for the purpose we are discussing here, is the concealed hammer design revolver; such as the S&W 642, and similar type models from that company, as well as the Ruger LCR and related models from that concern, plus comparable handguns from other manufacturers.

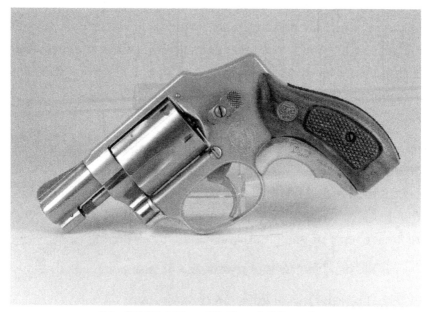

My S&W 642 ~ .38 Special Revolver

The lack of an exposed hammer offers a number of positive benefits for the average user;

No debris, lint, dirt or other unwanted material can enter the handgun's mechanism through the hammer opening, there being none.

The handgun is limited to a double-action pull of the trigger. A deliberate movement that is virtually impossible to accomplish by chance, accident, or unthinking error.

*

Where to Carry the Concealed Handgun?

There are three primary areas of the body where a person can conceal a handgun;

> ➢ Waist ~ Leg ~ Upper body

Depending on the typical living situation a user finds themselves in; their lifestyle, customary daily social interactions, usual attire worn and whether or not there is the need to ensure absolute concealment (as with an educator, physician, attorney, and most people working in "normal" businesses), will dictate, to a great extent, how a firearm is best (most practically) worn by that person. Whatever option is chosen will likely be a compromise between concealment, comfort, handgun size and cartridge power.

Before we discuss the three main areas where a person can conceal a handgun, I'd like to again go over what size handgun the user will most likely be armed with. The general rule of thumb, in regard which firearm is suitable for concealed carry, tends to revolve around size and weight. There are a couple of guidelines you should be aware of:

The larger the handgun (within reason and all else being equal);

> ➤ The easier its controls will be to operate.
> ➤ The more accurate the handgun will be for the user.
> ➤ The more potent the round it may be chambered for.
> ➤ The more rounds it will be able to carry.

It is also fair to state that, the larger the handgun;

> ➤ The more difficult the weapon will be to conceal.
> ➤ The less comfortable the gun will be to carry for any length of time.

From time to time I've heard people, when discussing this subject, utter a statement, something along the lines of, "You need to dress around the gun." In other words, the attire you wear must be secondary to, and in consideration of, the handgun you ought to carry. That advice, while sounding good, is just too simplistic a response to the question at hand, as well as being downright impractical for most people to abide by.

I've also heard some folks argue that the handgun you should routinely carry had best be nothing less than a full service size and caliber handgun, their argument being, if you're going to need a firearm for protection, it'd better be a "real" gun.

My response to the above is, it depends. If you normally wear clothing and operate in a work environment that is suitable for the comfortable carrying and concealment of a forty ounce handgun, plus an extra magazine of ammunition if it's a semi-auto, a full reload of shells if a revolver, if you have undergone the necessary training to safely carry such a pistol, and routinely undergo retraining with this sidearm, then by all means, that's the handgun for you.

As mentioned earlier, for most of my twenty years in the NYPD I wore two weighty revolvers (yes, I am aware I'm dating myself here) plus other "stuff" which totaled around five pounds on my waist. That's a lot of weight to routinely carry around, unless that individual is involved in aggressive law enforcement. But at the time it was appropriate to my work needs, how I dressed, and with who I interacted on a normal daily basis. Or, saying it another way, the equipment I wore was both *Practical* and *Task Related*.

So, prior to a discussion as to which sidearm you're going to arm yourself with, and how you plan on carrying it, some soul searching would be in order. Ask yourself;

- ➢ What kind of work do I do?
- ➢ How important is it be for my handgun to remain concealed while I'm at my job?
- ➢ How do I dress during normal social situations?
- ➢ What sort of people do I normally interact with?

Yes, a full-size Glock .40 S&W caliber handgun would be a fine choice for a defensive pistol, but could you comfortably (and practically) carry one during all the waking hours of the day?

As just mentioned, when with the NYPD (and when mostly as a detective) I carried two large handguns. Now, retired, I carry a small, lightweight, five round revolver in my pants pocket. Would I prefer to have a larger, heavier, more powerful, and accurate pistol with me in the event I encounter a serious threat to my life? Of course I would! It's just that a service size sidearm is no longer *Practical* for me to carry nor is it *Task Related* to my current daily needs.

Believe me when I tell you, if you opt to procure a handgun that is too large for comfortable daily wear, you'll soon stop carrying it. And that defeats the whole purpose of the exercise.

One other fact about handgun weight which is important to keep in mind; the lighter the firearm for a given caliber, the more intense the felt recoil. There is no free lunch here. With reduced weight comes a more snappy recoil impulse.

*

Differences Between Men and Women

The above section heading, while not the most artfully worded, brings us to the discussion of those issues which impede the comfortable carrying of handguns due to normal physiological and anatomical differences among people as well as those found between the two sexes.

For one thing, women tend to be "hippy." That is, from their waist down it is not uncommon, indeed, it's perfectly normal, for the female hip to bulge out a bit. This presents a dilemma for many women when attempting to carry a sidearm around the waist, particularly if concealment is important.

Guys, while not having to deal with the hip issue, often, especially with age, have their tummies sticking out, the proverbial "beer belly." Again, should waist area concealment be desired, depending on the holster/area the gun is to be carried, such an issue could cause a dilemma.

A woman's breast size can serve to either inhibit or enhance concealment around the upper chest area, depending on the type concealment holster desired to be worn.

Women's attire, dependent on the work they are performing, and how they socialize, can offer up both positive and negative concerns when it comes to concealing the handgun.

There are specialty holsters designed to be worn attached to a woman's brassiere. Here's a photo of one such model, the Looper FlashBang holster.

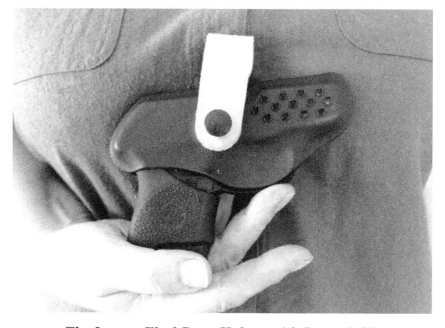

The Looper FlashBang Holster with Ruger LCP.

If pants are routinely worn then a strong side pocket carry option would be quite practical for a woman to utilize. Whatever the eventual solution to the most comfortable way to carry a handgun, please don't consider a purse as an option. I went into my objections to this mode of carry in an earlier chapter, so won't repeat my warnings here. Bottom line; it's a bad idea!

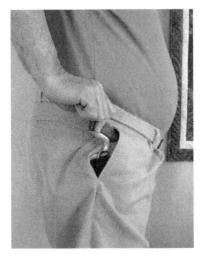 

A Handgun, concealed in a Pocket Holster, is Very Practical

Pocket Carry

From a tactical point of view wearing a handgun inside the strong side pants pocket, when worn with a good quality pocket holster, holds a number of advantages for the average person. Please note that any handgun so carried <u>must</u> be worn inside a pocket holster. You can't simply stick a pistol in your pocket and expect good concealment or wearer comfort. Furthermore, eventually your clothes will be ripped apart by the heavy metal object rubbing against the pocket's comparatively frail cloth. Besides protecting the pants pocket from wearing through due to the weight of the pistol, such a holster is also required in order to keep dirt and lint out of the firearm's mechanism, to ensure the weapon's maximum concealability, as well as prevent the handgun from flopping around and "printing" (being seen as a visible outline) through the fabric. Securing your handgun in your pants pocket also means the gun is routinely and normally much closer to the hand, thus weapon access will likely be more rapid and secure.

The downside of pocket carry is, this location severely limits the size of the handgun worn. As a practical matter, once a handgun reaches around twenty ounces in weight, the comfortable and practical carrying of such a size firearm in the pocket becomes problematic.

Properly worn, pocket type holsters can be very discreet. The pants shown in the photo of pocket holster carry are summer weight. With a heavier fabric there is virtually no outline of the handgun visible.

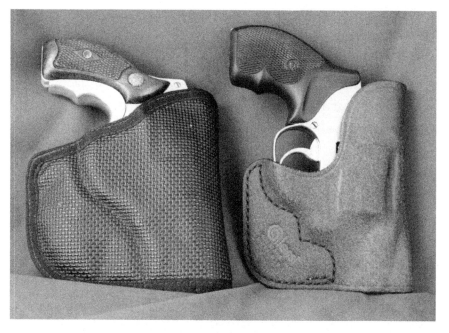

Two Pocket Holsters a DeSantis Nemises and an Alessi

The two materials pocket holsters are generally made from are leather or, alternatively, some synthetic (Kydex is common). I've used both and, properly designed, both types of material serve well. The goal of the pocket holster is to act as a pouch, not to offer any retention off the handgun. You don't want the attempted withdrawal of the sidearm to result in the drawing of a holstered handgun!

The pocket holster has a significant tactical advantage over other type of handgun concealment locations; no one knows that you are armed, including any potential threat you are facing, even if you have your hand on your sidearm! As a civilian, you cannot "brandish" your handgun if you simply "think" you are facing some threat to your life. The tactical advantage therefore is almost always on the side of the potential assailant, as that person must, by law, make the first threatening move before you are justified in exposing your handgun. With front pocket carry, your hand can be on your revolver, unseen by all around you, but ready if needed for immediate protection of your life. That is a tremendous advantage and one which should not be discounted.

*

The Belt, Again

Don't discount the need for a good belt when wearing your handgun in your pocket. You'd be surprised how the weight of even a small handgun, along with all the other "stuff" normally carried in the pocket, tends to pull the pants down. The solution is to wear a good quality combat belt. If for some reason that's not practical, or desired (there being some social "need" to wear a dress belt, for example), consider wearing suspenders to assist in bearing the weight of the firearm. I've opted to use suspenders often when compelled to carry a weighty handgun in my pants pocket. They really do help.

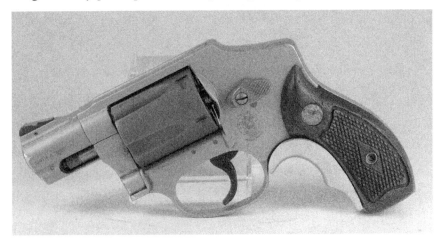

S&W Model 342 ~ Very Lightweight, & Heavy Recoil, .38 Special!!

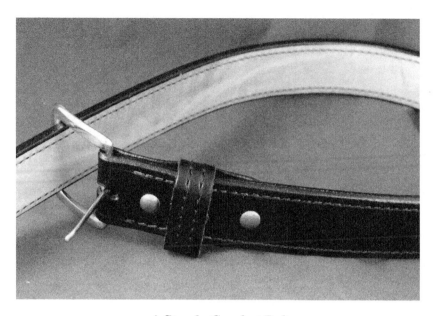

A Sturdy Combat Belt

<u>Other Options</u>

If your normal attire permits, carrying a sidearm in a well-constructed holster, attached to a good quality combat belt, is hard to beat. This includes strong-side carry and cross draw designs. The advantages of such a setup is that you can carry a larger, service size handgun, quite comfortably. Naturally, in order to conceal the handgun in this manner you must always be wearing a jacket or some sort of outermost garment.

Many people like to conceal their handgun with an inside the waistband holster (IWB). A well-made design of this type can prove quite useful.

Two pieces of advice. First, and I know this is counterintuitive, a two-inch barrel revolver is harder to conceal with the IWB holster (this goes for the strong sided outside waistband holster as well) than a three inch or longer barrel handgun. The longer barrel, pushing against the body, serves to press the butt of the handgun against the user's body, enhancing concealment. Since the IWB design already conceals the handgun, there is no negative associated to the wearing of the longer barrel. There is the bonus of increased muzzle velocity as well.

For the record I've carried, extensively, my S&W model 10, four-inch heavy barrel revolver, as well as a Colt 1911A1, using the IWB design. This type holster is both very concealable as well as being comfortable, if a good quality design is chosen.

Should you wish to consider such a model please avoid a cheap version that uses a metal clip to retain the holster to the belt. This is for two reasons; the metal clip designs tend to be destructive to clothing, and, far worse, this type of clip design tends NOT to hold the holster in place when the gun is withdrawn.

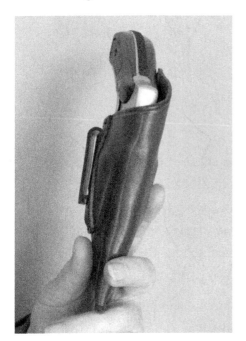 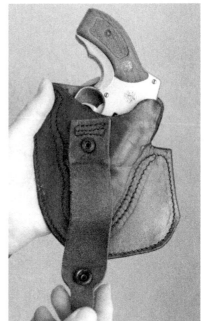

Alessi IWB on Left, DeSantis with Leather Belt Loop on Right

The Alessi IWB shown has a very secure and well-designed plastic retaining clip. The DeSantis holster shown uses a leather loop to secure the holster to the gunbelt.

The crossdraw holster is not as popular as the strong side type. Having used both (often at the same time when involved in active law enforcement) I have found the cross draw to be useful in that the gun is readily available when seated (as in an automobile), and it offers the added advantage of not telegraphing the user's intent of going for a handgun as readily as does the strong side carry holster.

Some folks like small of the back carry (so-called SOB). If it works for you, great. I suspect access to the firearm, while seated, might be problematic. Also, comfort when seated could be an issue.

*

I'd be remiss if not mentioning one other possible means of concealing a handgun around the waist area, the "belly band" type holster. Actually, there are a number of similar designs; there is the "pure" belly band, which is a wrap that goes around the mid-section of the body and which has a pouch sewn in it for a handgun. Another comparable type of holster wraps around the waist and the handgun is dropped in its pouch, named Thunderwear or Smartwear.

The handgun rests underneath the wearer's pants, directly in front of the groin area. I've used several of this design and they offer excellent concealment and comfort, rapid access to your firearm and the ability, depending on the wearer's body type, to conceal a fairly large pistol.

*

Ankle Holsters

A good quality ankle holster is an excellent way to conceal a firearm. Both men and women, when wearing slacks, can comfortably go about while armed, yet have a useable and practical size handgun on their person. This is the primary advantage of the ankle holster and, depending on the type of work environment you find yourself in, may be the best answer, for you, to the problem of how to conceal a handgun.

A person can comfortably carry a compact but service-size pistol in an ankle holster and walk around the office in shirt sleeves with no one being the wiser. This design is a great way to access a handgun if you're seated. The problem with this mode of carry is, it's not so good when you're standing. Do keep in mind this design's limitations. Under normal circumstances the ankle holster would not be the ideal location to conceal a handgun. Should it be needed in an emergency the user must do one of two things; either bend down to retrieve the sidearm or, raise the leg which holds the ankle holster while standing on one leg.

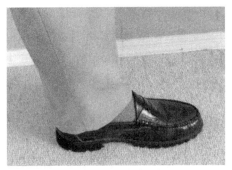

My S&W 642 Seen Exposed and When Under a Pant Leg

For the record I've carried a Glock 19, which, when loaded, weighs approximately thirty-three ounces, in an ankle holster all day with complete comfort. I've also carried, from time to time, my back-up Colt Detective Special (of similar weight) in an ankle holster. The gun was secure even during police chases and while climbing over fences.

One last issue that needs consideration in regard ankle carry; the gun so worn will be close to the ground and thus susceptible to picking up dust and debris more readily than other holster designs. This is of particular concern should the user opt to carry a small, semi-auto pistol. I've found such handguns far more likely to malfunction due to ankle carry.

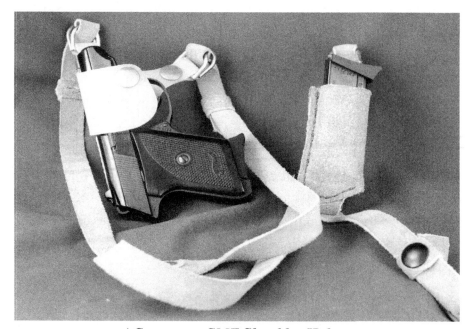

***A Seventrees SMZ Shoulder Holster
with a Walther TPH .22 long rifle Pistol***

Shoulder Holsters

The chest area is where the shoulder holster comes into play. Some people swear by them, others find them uncomfortable to wear. None the less, they look sexier than heck. I mean, all those tough TV and movie cops wear one, right?

Finding a really good quality shoulder rig is somewhat problematic. Ideally, for comfort a shoulder holster should be custom fit to the user. Finding a professional holster maker able to do such a fitting is a near impossibility for most people.

I've found that as a practical matter a shoulder rig can be used – comfortably– with a handgun that weighs in at around twenty-five ounces or so. I prefer the design which holds the sidearm horizontal to the ground, with the handgun's butt in a position for immediate access to the user. Whether standing or seated the handgun can be easily drawn.

The photo on the previous page is an example of a truly exotic holster. Made by the long defunct Seventrees Holster Company, of New York City, it was designed for use by intelligence agents who carried "suppressed" (silenced) pistols. The "silencer" would attach to the gun's muzzle yet not interfere with the weapon's removal from the shoulder rig. The pistol would be pushed up and twisted outward in order to release it from the snap on its plastic retainer.

The design worked well and was very lightweight, a truly minimalist holster. It required the user to be sure they knew what they were doing as the pistol's trigger would, by the nature of the design, press up against the snap release on withdrawal. A lawyer's nightmare (or perhaps dream…).

Exotic holsters may be of some use, again depending on your specific needs and practical limitations. If possible, I suggest you stay with time proven designs that are comfortable to wear for long periods of time.

*

I would like to take a moment in order to explain what I meant earlier by a "good quality" holster and combat belt.

A concealment holster should be constructed of quality cow or (better yet) horse hide, designed, and molded, for the specific firearm to be carried in it. There are a number of excellent custom holster makers now offering good, solid designs. A combat belt is a belt made from two pieces of either cow or horse hide, of a suitable width for the weight of the handgun to be carried (I found a 1¼" width belt is about right for a service weight pistol although many experienced firearms carriers prefer the 1½" size) and stitched along its length with nylon thread.

The size of the belt loop on the holster should exactly match the size of the belt's width. The holster should be held in place securely when it's attached to the belt, with no flop or play. That is how a professional carries a handgun on their person.

Under no circumstances, and I mean *NONE*, can you opt to keep firearms "locked-up" in a secure location for availability in "an emergency." You can never know when, or where, an emergency requiring the immediate access to a firearm will take place. The only secure way to ensure a sidearm will be available is to have the firearm on your person. Thus, the only places appropriate for a handgun is either worn on the body, or secured in a safe.

You must understand, when circumstances arise that pose a life-threatening situation, you have very little time to react. Life does not play out as is portrayed in the movies or on television. No one is going to hand you a script prior to you having to confront an exigent, life threatening situation. Bad things happen very, very quickly, and most unexpectantly.

On the next page are two examples of quality, small frame revolvers, a Smith and Wesson (S&W) model 642, and the S&W model 60, both five shot, .38 Special caliber revolvers, in pocket holsters. They are both well-made handguns. Their primary advantage, and main disadvantage, is one of size. Although easy to carry and conceal, this type of handgun (and those of similar size and power) are far more difficult to learn to master.

S&W Model 60, with Customized Bobbed Hammer

Two "J-Frame" S&W Handguns in Pocket Holsters

While it is true that a skilled and practiced shooter can fire such a size handgun with credible and practical accuracy, their light weight, rather robust recoil, and small grip, make hitting one's intended target something of a chore.

On the next page is a target I shot during a night qualification while chief of police with the Wellfleet Police Department (a small town located on Cape Cod). As I was not carrying my personal handgun during the exercise, I borrowed another officer's S&W model 642 in order to fire the course. Ranges fired were five, ten and fifteen yards distance, using service ammunition.

The Author's Colt Detective Special, Worn While in NYPD

Photo of my S&W 642 Night Qualification Target

While a small handgun can be fired with credible accuracy, this takes a great deal of training and practice to accomplish.

*

A Handful of "Exotic Designs

Here are a few more interesting (in my opinion) holsters, presented simply to show the reader what's possible in concealment holsters. The design on the next page is one I sketched out with Ken Null (of Null Holsters) doing the actual leather work. It's a hip-pocket holster for my .22 long rifle caliber Walther TPH with room for an extra magazine.

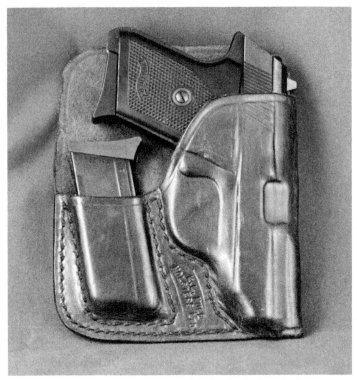

A Null Hip Pocket Holster of my Design

A High-Standard D-101 .22 Magnum Derringer in a Custom Holster

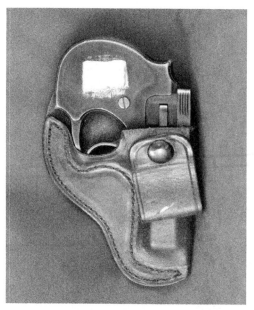

The small holster seen here are for my Hi-Standard model 101, .22 Magnum, two shot derringer (long since out of manufacture). This very flat pistol used an exposed trigger and fired two rounds of that rather potent little .22 Magnum rimfire round.

The duct-tape, while not attractive, was most functional in keeping dirt out of the little pistol's mechanism.

An Interesting Little Pistol, a Hi-Standard Model 101, .22 Magnum

The two derringers in the picture seen on the next page are how they normally look before I took off the grips for added compactness. After my little "modification" they appear like the version seen above. The ugly (but functional) duct-tape was placed on both sides of the open grip panels, where holes would otherwise permit debris from entering the small handgun.

I only had one call to carry this gun while working as an NYPD detective. I was the "chum" waiting inside a bank for a robbery team to hit, and this little gun was to be my last-ditch defense if the situation became critical. Fortunately, the gun wasn't needed, and we captured the four robbers (in the middle of them robbing the bank!) without incident a week or so later.

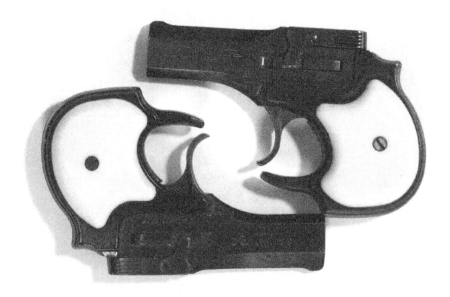

This is how the Hi-Standard Derringers (Model 100, in .22 long rifle and Model 101, in .22 Magnum) Look Before my "Modification."

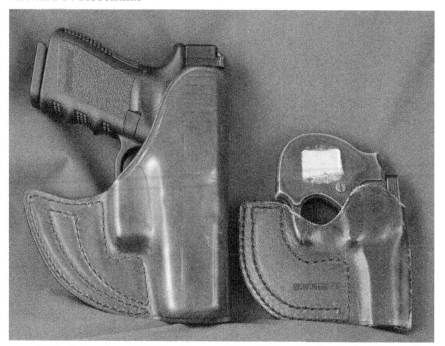

***A Null Pocket Holster for my Glock 19 and an Old Seventrees
Pocket Holster for my Hi-Standard Derringer.***

Finally, above are two pocket holsters that demonstrate the extremes possible with this design. The larger one is for my Glock 19, the "petite" model is an old Seventrees holster, made for the Hi-Standard Derringer. Neither holster is particularly practical (the smaller one because of the nature of the little handgun), although I will admit to having worn the Seventrees design on more than a few occasions, slipping it into my hip pocket.

Lastly, as a general rule I urge you not to try to save money by purchasing inexpensive gear. A quality holster and belt combination, purchased from a high quality custom maker, will last you many years, and will be comfortable and concealable. It might also save your life someday.

Firearms and the Home

Myths of Armed Self-Defense

Common misconceptions regarding self-defense as well as a discussion on some basic tactics to employ while at home

I was unsure whether or not to include this material in the book. But so many people have, over the years, asked me the same questions, and seem to take to heart the same myths in regard firearms and their use, that I felt compelled to add this chapter. My former boss at the Firearms and Tactics Section, Lieutenant Frank McGee, used to say that teaching a person how to use a firearm, without teaching them when to use it, was only giving them "half a loaf." Therefore, while this book may be titled *A Practical Guide to Handgun Firearms Training,* I believe I'd be remiss in not addressing, at least to a limited degree, the "when and how" to use the firearm should the need arise when at home.

During many a social conversation I've listened to a number of myths, the same one's repeated time after time, in regard the most appropriate way an armed, law abiding citizen, should handle home defense situations. Most of these suggestions were, at best, specious, and at worst likely to get those who follow such guidance into a great deal of legal trouble. We'll examine a few now:

If you find an intruder in your home you can shoot him.

There are a number of variables that should be considered before a person ought to resort to the use of deadly physical force. One of the most important considerations is, what are your state's laws in regard this matter! Because this book is written as a general guide, I'm compelled to discuss this subject as a broad overview. A few initial thoughts in regard the use of deadly physical force are:

> ➢ What are the specific circumstances the homeowner is facing? And,
> ➢ What is the level of the perceived threat?

Just because there is stranger in your home does not automatically mean you have a license to shoot them! Some of the constraints which face a home's resident are:

> Age and physical condition of the inhabitants in your home.
> Who was the initial aggressor during the incident?
> Are there any weapons visible?
> Is the homeowner in fear of bodily harm?

Is the person standing before you a neighborhood child who simply wandered in to your house, an inebriated adult who picked the wrong place to sleep it off, or a burglar intent on committing a serious crime? Before a person can lawfully use deadly physical force (or lethal force, which has the same meaning) another the general rule to follow, really a question, is, is the homeowner in fear for his or her life, or the life of an innocent third party?

While it is theoretically possible for the use of deadly physical force to be justified when the user of the force was the person who initiated the confrontation, such a fact pattern would make it very difficult to demonstrate that the lawful use of force was applied. If there is a guest present at your residence, and you, the homeowner, initiated some argument or physical confrontation, then attempted to back out of the fray, only to have to resort to the use of deadly physical force, whether or not you can legally prevail in such a matter is open to question.

Most confrontations of this sort, which involve the use of a firearm for personal protection, take place during the hours of darkness. That is the reason experienced firearms instructors suggest that beside the handgun (or whatever firearm is being used for home security) there should be a high-quality flashlight nearby.

The mental state of the homeowner at the time of the encounter is another consideration. Is that person up and awake and totally aware of their surroundings? Indeed, when you are woken at some early hour, how alert and clear thinking are you? As a responsible citizen you cannot afford to take an action at the level of the use of deadly physical force, without having a clear understanding of, as well as a clearly defined and identified target, in regard the threat you are facing.

Flashlights

Target identification brings us to the subject of flashlights, and which technique is best used when employing a light during a possible deadly physical force situation. There are two fundamental schools of thought on how to actually hold the flashlight; either in close proximity to the shooting hand, adding some support and stability to the firing position, or, independent of the shooter's gun hand, up and away from the shooter's body. The FBI prefers the latter technique (or, at least the last time I heard this was still their protocol), many other agencies lean toward the former style. Let's discuss these variations a bit.

Some years earlier I was reading an article in a popular firearm and related equipment-oriented magazine. The article discussed which firearms/flashlight technique was best. Photos of no less than two dozen styles were shown, most having just the most subtle of variation between them, and each carrying the name of their "inventor." No self-interest there, I'm sure.

If you use one of the "modern" style techniques, which requires you to place the flashlight and firearm in close proximity, both held directly in front of the face when aiming at the target, the main points you should understand are;

> ➢ If performed correctly, these techniques give additional support to your shooting hand.
> ➢ You will have the handgun and the flashlight pointed at the same location prior to discharging the piece.
> ➢ Bad guys know about this style. They'll likely shoot at the light, which will be directly in front of you.

Should you prefer to use the "older" style technique, the flashlight held high, away from and in front of the shooter's body, the considerations are;

> The light is some distance from and forward of the body.
> 1-Keep the light ahead of the body so that no part of the body is illuminated by it (at least when you are in the "ready" position.)
> 2-With this technique, someone shooting at the light will likely miss you.
> This style does not offer the same firing stability as does the two-handed technique.

Commonly Referred to as the FBI Technique

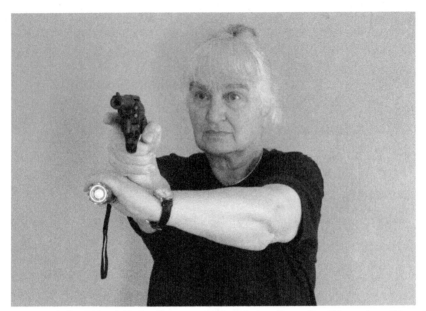

Use of the Flashlight Support Hand Against the Shooting Hand

There are dozens of supported flashlight technics to choose from.

Whichever style you opt to use remember not to operate the light as you would normally use a flashlight (by just turning, and leaving, it on). This broadcasts to anyone hiding in the dark where you are. The proper tactical use of the light is in short bursts. Furthermore, unless you find yourself routinely involved in armed night operations, I would urge you learn, use and master a single technique.

Keep in mind that it would be most prudent, before any other activity is undertaken, to first know where all the home's inhabitants are located before engaging in a "search and destroy" mission. Should you suspect there is an intruder in the home, if at all possible, bring everyone into one room (the master bedroom is a good place). Once there, have everyone take cover. If there is an intruder in the home, they must come through the door of the master bedroom before they can do anyone any harm. This puts the bad guy in the neck of a visual funnel. That door will be your primary point of attention during this event.

Flashlight or no, do not go looking for the intruder! You've likely just woken up, are a bit disorientated, undoubtedly nervous, frightened and upset, as well as lightly dressed. You have no idea how many people you are dealing with, or what their capabilities and intentions are.

Police must be called –use 911– as soon as practical. Depending on where you live (and the professional level of your local police) will determine the response time to your residence. In rural areas, it might take officers an hour to arrive (really). In my little town on Cape Cod, perhaps three to five minutes, maybe a bit longer.

A knowledgeable burglar will know that the unhooking of any hard-wired phone in the home will render all phones there useless. This is the main reason I like to keep my cell phone by my bed.

One question you might ask yourself is, how do you expect responding officers to enter your home once they get there? I urge my students to affix a house-key to a large white, or at least a light, brightly colored plastic container lid, or some similar object. You want to use such a large white lid or colorful piece of plastic because this is what your house-key will be affixed to (which will be kept in a draw next to your bed) when you toss the key to the responding officers from your bedroom window (especially important if the master bedroom is on the second floor). It will be dark out and the officers will need to be able to locate the house key quickly. Otherwise the only way the officers could gain entry into the home would be by breaking in themselves!

*

Some Common Myths

> ➢ If you shoot an intruder who turns out to be unarmed, arm them!

Beside the ethical and moral dilemma such an act places you in, the problem with the above "advice" is that if you put a "weapon" by an intruder's body, and it later comes out that you did so, your entire defense of justification, which may have been otherwise perfectly legitimate, may be in jeopardy.

Please understand, burglars frequently enter homes unarmed, then pick up a weapon once inside the house. Often, they'll go into the family's "arsenal" (the kitchen) for a large knife. I've also known such criminals to find for themselves baseball bats, fireplace pokers or any other impact weapons they may come across. Police are aware of this. It is common, at the scene of burglaries, for officers to find such objects lying near where the burglar exited the residence.

From a tactical point of view, it would be prudent for you, as the lawful resident of the home, to reasonably believe that the person standing, uninvited, in front of you at 2:30 in the morning, is armed with some sort of weapon.

> If the burglar has fallen outside the home, drag him inside

Dragging a body from outside the house back inside after you've shot them? Really? How many dead human bodies have you ever moved? Especially after you've just killed that person? What state of mind do you think you'd be in after such an event? How clearly would your thoughts be at that moment? You don't think the responding officers, and certainly the forensic technicians, will see that a body has been moved from where it first fell? Indeed, the trail of blood, shoe scrape marks, the way the body lies, all these variables will tell a tale. And, here again, what might have been the perfectly lawful use of deadly physical force now comes into question.

As an aside, be as accurate as you can recall in regard your distance from the perpetrator at the moment you discharged your firearm. A forensic pathologist can readily determine –to within a few inches– how far away you were when the shot was fired. This is a well-established science. The stippling of burned and unburned powder particles forms a shotgun-like pattern on both skin and clothing. The diameter of the marks made will show the distance from the muzzle of the firearm which made them.

> If you shoot a perpetrator, make sure they're dead

How many times I've heard this nonsensical fable bandied about by wannabe "tough guys." Yes, it is true that injured perpetrators of criminal acts (due to a victim's gunfire or some other act of legitimate self-defense) have won substantial judgments (although this possibility varies greatly from state to state and is pretty remote). Some states offer victims of crimes substantial legal protections in the event force is used to thwart a bona fide home or business invasion, or to prevent some other crime.

Back to this myth. Should you opt to shoot an individual who is already lying on the ground (in an effort to make sure they are dead) you will be firing at this person from a very unique angle. The path your projectile will take will be quite different than when you fired on them when they were standing. Forensic technicians are trained to look for such anomalies. Once again, what might have been a legitimate act of self-defense on your part will be put in serious question.

> After you shoot a mugger, if there are no witnesses, take off!

Should you do such a thing, and are found out, the first question the enforcement authorities will have is, if you were innocent, why did you flee the scene?

Some years ago, there was a most unfortunate case in New York City. A gentleman by the name of Frank Magliato was involved in a motor vehicle accident. The other person involved, a dangerously violent individual, was, at one point in the confrontation, armed with a police style baton. The facts of the case are complex, and if you are interested may read an excellent synopsis at the web site I've listed in this chapter's Reference Section in regard this incident.[1]

The substance of the case is that a licensed New York City pistol permit holder (Magliato), after being attacked by a man with a club, and while clearly in danger of being the victim of a deadly physical force attack, fired a round that ended the confrontation. He panicked, fled the scene, and, at trial, was sentenced to fifteen years to life in prison for what should have otherwise been adjudicated to be a justifiable self-defense shooting.

Keep in mind, in a shooting situation you develop tunnel vision. You would not be living out some scene being acted out as in a movie. Rather, a gunfight is a highly emotional, gut wrenching, life-changing event. You will never see all the witnesses around you during the incident. You will never be aware of the ubiquitous surveillance cameras documenting the event. If you flee that very act will be interpreted as "guilt." Know your rights, avail yourself of them once the police arrive (to mostly remain silent), but stay at the scene.

> ➤ I couldn't ever really shoot anyone – I have the gun just to scare people away from me

This is a very dangerous attitude for the armed law-abiding citizen to have. There is no way to predetermine the mindset of a person you might face during a life-threatening confrontation. It has been my experience that a significant number of criminals have, to varying degree, mental health issues. The vast majority do not, as a matter of course, make good life decisions. The mindset, and resultant actions, of such folks kept me gainfully employed for over forty years as a law enforcement officer.

If you are facing a street level mugger, it is likely that person is little more than an entrepreneur (OK, a violent entrepreneur). That's a fancy way of saying they're in it for the money. Robbery is not a sport to them (generally), or some sort of a lark, but rather a way to ensure a redistribution of wealth; i.e., your wealth transferred to them. Such criminals seek out compliant victims. There is little to gain by them when going up against an armed, and determined, adversary. But the criminal <u>must believe</u> that you have the internal will to deal with him. If you are not mentally and emotionally prepared to use your firearm when necessary in the defense of your life or the life of an innocent third party, you are better off not carrying a firearm.

> ➤ The key to successful armed self-defense is the right gun/ammunition combination

There is no magic firearm or cartridge that a person can possess for personal defense. You cannot "buy" your way to firearms handling competency by simply purchasing expensive equipment. You must receive hands-on training in the use of your firearm, the use of force, tactical considerations to be employed during the use of force, as well as when you may lawfully use such force, plus what you ought to say after you've used deadly physical force (generally, the best thing to say is, not much).

When carrying a concealed firearm there is the inevitable compromise between portability and concealability. Many variables apply here. Certainly, the largest concealable handgun a person can comfortably and reasonably carry would be best. The larger the handgun, the easier it is to hit one's intended target, plus such sidearms are chambered for more powerful rounds. None the less, when I'm heading down to the local grocery with my wife's "honey-do" list, it is unlikely that I'll be dressed in a manner which would permit me to arm myself with an optimum size handgun. More often than not I'll have on my person a five shot, S&W revolver, carried in a suitable holster in my front pants pocket.

Different situations call for different solutions. I have a dear friend, a senior member of a large city law firm. He travels daily, by subway, to his office, carrying a Walther PPK in his outermost garment pocket. When he gets to his law office, he takes the small handgun and puts it in his ankle holster, where it remains until he leaves for the day.

Certainly, a service size handgun would have been the better gun to have, but the social and business situation my friend faces makes that choice impossible. In my opinion, given his options, he made a wise decision.

Whatever firearm circumstances limit you to carry, make sure you know how to use it. In addition, keep firmly in mind that accurate bullet placement is the ultimate in stopping power.

> ➤ Don't draw your firearm unless you're going to pull the trigger

I've pulled my handgun from its holster hundreds of times while in the NYPD. I've pulled the trigger once in the line of duty, to save another person's life.

When you draw your firearm, you should be legally justified in doing so and emotionally prepared to fire it. You should be tactically aware of what you are doing in the context of the situation you are in. Much of the time, the mere act of drawing a weapon is sufficient to end the confrontation. Remember, muggers are like business men; they're in it for the money, not for the sport.

*

The House Gun

> ➤ Yes or No?
> ➤ Safety at home
> ➤ Liabilities: Criminal and Civil
> ➤ Use of tactics
> ➤ Security of firearms at home
> ➤ Safety at Home

Clearly, by the very fact that you're reading this book shows you are predisposed to have at least one firearm in the home. The question of the "house-gun" raises issues that are part philosophical, part legal, and part practical. There is no single correct answer. For example, do you have children at home? What are their ages, personalities, social interactions, disabilities, proclivities, etc.? What about other adults in the home? Are any with emotional problems, are they immature, do they have issues with drugs or alcohol? These are tough questions, but germane to the matter at hand.

Once you've decided that a firearm would be an asset, who in the home will have both knowledge of the firearm's location as well as access to the gun? If this person is your spouse, will they be interested in taking some training with you in order to learn how to properly and safely operate the firearm?

Some suggest that a firearm in the home is not the way to ensure the family's protection. I've heard it stated that, in the event of a problem, just call the police!?! After all, that's what we pay them for. Well, I'd like to offer up two reasons why this answer might not be wholly satisfactory;

1-When seconds count the police will take several minutes to get to you, and,

2-The police are under no legal obligation to protect you.

Time is not your friend during an emergency situation. Here's one example below:

December 17, 2011

In a crisis, Chloe Symington's dad told her, "think now, react or panic later."

That advice was running through her mind when the 13-year-old Michigan girl grabbed her cat, hid in her bedroom and phoned 911 about two intruders' downstairs in her family's home Thursday.

"I was just curled up in a ball right there," said Chloe, pointing at a corner as she recalled what happened to <u>ABC affiliate WXYZ in Detroit.</u>

Two to three minutes passed between her sighting of the intruders rifling through the drawers of a downstairs table and one of them actually entering her bedroom.

"I was really freaked out," she added.

But during an 18-minute, 911 call, she remained outwardly calm, speaking quietly.

"How did they not see you??" the 911 operator asked, while Chloe crawled under the bed.

"I don't know Chloe," told her.

"Just lay quiet," the operator said.

Chloe's action helped put officers from Macomb County Sheriff Department police near the scene before Daniel Laflin and Michael Zdanukiewicz, both 19, could fully get away with the electronics and a handgun they had stolen from the Symington family's home.

They were arraigned on home invasion charges.

*

Here we have a young woman who, during a burglary in progress, had to wait **eighteen minutes** for the police to arrive. This is not uncommon. The small Cape Cod town I live in, Wellfleet, is nine miles long. It has an excellent police department. An officer, upon receiving the call for assistance from dispatch (a process that may well take a minute of give and take communication between the complainant and the dispatcher) may be seven to ten minutes away from arriving at the problem location, even should they be driving at a faster than normal rate of speed. At sixty miles per hour an eight-mile ride would take the officer eight minutes, assuming they could find the location immediately (more than a few of the homes here are situated on sand roads first laid out in the seventeen hundreds!).

Get it into your head; during an emergency, at least for the initial few minutes, you are on your own!

<u>The police are under no legal obligation to protect individuals</u>

This is a difficult concept for most folks to accept, but it is fact. The United Stated Supreme Court has ruled that the police are under no constitutionally mandated duty to protect a person from harm.[2] In that case a woman with a signed court-issued order of protection, lost her three children –they were murdered– by her estranged husband, yet the court found that the police were under no constitutional duty or obligation in the matter to protect her or her children (Castle Rock v. Gonzales).

There are some exceptions. One exists if there is a "special relationship" between the police and a person, or, if there is a state-created danger.[3] None the less, there have been some disturbing incidents involving police (and fire department) failures to act, with no consequences to any of the responders involved. In one particularly grotesque case, both police and fire personnel simply watched a man commit suicide by drowning because the police and fire officers were in a budget dispute with their city.[4] On Memorial Day, 2011, a suicidal man in San Francisco Bay stood in the water for an hour while onlookers begged the responding police and fire units to do something! When the man finally drowned it took a bystander to retrieve the body, as the fire personnel stated that their budget had not permitted them to have proper cold-water rescue training!

Fortunately, most responding police (and fire) officers don't comport themselves as did the rather sad examples I mentioned above. None the less the reality is, for all practical purposes, your immediate personal safety is in your hands.

OK, we want a house gun! Now what?

Keep in mind, we're still discussing the "house-gun" here. So, we need to determine, what type firearm is most suited for the purpose? Handgun or long arm (rifle or shotgun)?

The deciding factor is more a matter of how committed a person is to receiving professional training (no, training is not simply popping some rounds off down at the local sand pit!)? Firearms are complex mechanisms, some types more so than others. All require hands-on, structured instruction in their proper use. "My buddy showed me how to use it," or, "My dad took me to the range a couple of times," is woefully insufficient training to meet your self-defense needs.

Most folks interested in firearms find kindred souls and are guided by their friends' views on the matter. However, unless these individuals are trained firearms instructors, more often than not bad information, along with unsafe and poor gun handling habits, are passed along. There are many fine firearms training venues available. I urge you to research those nearest to you and take advantage of the training offered!

At any rate, the problem with using a long arm for home self-defense is not that they are inferior to handguns for this purpose. On the contrary, virtually any long arm is superior to a handgun in both power and practical accuracy. But, for home defense purposes these types of firearm are difficult to safely secure, and keep out of sight, while still being kept in a ready condition when they are serving their home defense purpose. Some people do prefer long arms for home defense, and that's fine. But, for the purposes of our discussion, we'll limit the available options to handguns.

The least appropriate types of handgun for home defense are either the little snubby revolver "detective" gun, or a semi-automatic pistol which you are not thoroughly familiar with. Small revolvers are designed with concealment in mind. Sure, they do enjoy the benefit of looking "sexy," and, anyway, if our favorite cop heroes on TV can use them, why can't we? Well, for one thing, for the average shooter, when trying to hit anything with this type handgun people find it far more difficult to strike their target, plus these small handguns suffer a significant loss of power (velocity is reduced) due their short barrel length (a handgun firearm projectile's velocity increases with barrel length, right up to around the twelve to sixteen-inch mark).

For handguns, the service size semi-auto pistol is a superior self-defense tool. For the trained user this type sidearm permits more accurate fire, holds many more rounds than the revolver for a given caliber, and is an overall better handgun choice, if a viable option. The flip side of the coin is, these are complex mechanisms, frequently requiring the user to be able to manipulate, under adverse conditions, a number of small operating parts (safety, slide release, magazine release), as well as successfully clear the weapon should there be a malfunction or failure to fire. This is one of the reasons I harp on the need for professional training. To properly use such a sidearm requires that the users condition themselves (the term "muscle memory" is used in this regard) to be able to work the handgun without conscious thought. And we haven't even broached the subject of mastering clearance drills under stressful and in exigent circumstances.

For the average, occasional firearms user, for home defense purposes, I suggest they consider procuring a used police service revolver. Although you still must learn how to properly operate this type of sidearm, revolvers tend to be:

- ➤ Simpler to operate than semi-auto pistols
- ➤ Always ready for use as they contain no springs under maximum compression
- ➤ Require less maintenance
- ➤ Are very reliable
- ➤ Fairly inexpensive to purchase
- ➤ Safer in less experienced hands

Choice of caliber

This tends to be a contentious issue. Intensely interested firearms enthusiasts have their "favorites." Those who disagree often verbally engage in the debate with the same vigor as one often sees when one's sport team's prowess is questioned. And, to my way of thinking, such enthusiastic disagreements carry just about the same merit and utility as does the arguing over sporting events.

For our purposes (seeking out what is both *Practical* and *Task Related*) I would like to offer the following as a guide. For home protection:

For the revolver

> ➤ Any caliber of .38 Special power or greater should suffice.

For the semi-auto pistol

> ➤ A caliber of 9x19mm (9mm Luger) power, or greater, should suffice.

In either case, no more powerful round should be chosen unless the user can control its recoil. Remember, you can only fire your handgun as rapidly as you can successfully hit your target. Fast misses serve no purpose.

I urge my readers to use caution here. You may well be subjected to peer pressure in regard the "best" handgun round to use. Please disregard the nonsense you hear. Handguns tend to be low powered weapons. What effectiveness these firearms do have comes into play when the shooter is able to place their rounds in the high center of mass of an adversaries' chest. Any service size round will suffice, assuming high quality ammunition, appropriate to the task, is used. What I mean by this is, while the firing of substantial amounts of inexpensive full-jacket (or round nose lead) rounds for training is appropriate and even necessary (as the cost per round is lower than with service ammunition), for self-defense purposes it would be best to choose one of the rounds commonly used by law enforcement agencies for this purpose.

Richard P. Rosenthal

Projectile penetration concerns in the home

This is a legitimate concern. The average service handgun round, if fired inside the typical American's residence, can be expected to penetrate through most, if not all, of the home's walls. Consider this, it is common for our homes to be "stick-built," constructed with interior plasterboard walls. While perfectly suitable for the intended purpose, such materials offer little resistance to handgun projectiles, which will penetrate many such walls before coming to a stop.

In a roundabout way this is just a restatement of the safety warning that you have to know and identify your target, as well as know what's behind your target, before discharging your piece.

*

Liability concerns

While each state has their own set of laws in regard the use of deadly physical force, I'm going to generalize and state, so long as you are in your home, are in fear for your life (or the life of another innocent person), was not the initial aggressor, nor initiated the violent encounter, it is likely that you would be deemed within your lawful rights to use deadly physical force against an unlawful intruder.

I don't wish to go into great detail here in regard the lawful use of force. There are many fine books on the subject as well as training programs out there which you can take advantage of. Please consider the following material as an overview and introduction on the subject.

Some basic points you ought to consider and understand:

Under no set of circumstances are you ever authorized to "shoot to kill." I am unaware of any state law that gives its citizens the right and authority to intentionally take a human life. You *MAY* be legally permitted to use lethal force/deadly physical force, to protect yourself or another. It's not the same thing. The only entity with the lawful authority to take a human life in our nation is the government, but only after a trial, and while following the detailed process that such an act entails. As a citizen, in defense of your life, you have the right to _STOP_ the attack against you. In order to do this you may, depending on the facts of the situation, need to use the amount of deadly physical force necessary to terminate the assault on you (deadly physical force being that amount of force that is likely to cause death or serious physical injury). This is a most important distinction and one you should carefully consider.

It comes down to your intent. Did you "intend" to kill your adversary, thereby committing a non-justifiable homicide, or did you intend to simply stop your assailant, even though the end result also culminated in death.

The law looks at the actions we take (I'm keeping this much simplified here) based both on our intent as well as what we actually did. Sometimes bad things happen, but without criminal intent, yet with serious, sometimes fatal consequences. Automobile accidents are a prime example of horrific injuries resulting from an incident, with no criminal responsibility falling on any of the parties involved.

In order to be justified in the use of deadly physical force (or lethal force, as they are the same thing) three elements need be present;

- Ability to cause injury
- Proximity to the victim
- Manifest Intent to cause the harm

Permit me the use of a silly analogy to make my point. At a baseball game a player is up at bat. The player takes a full swing at the very same moment the umpire leans a bit too far forward. The bat strikes the umpire, causing serious physical injury. Clearly, we have ability (the batter was holding an object that could be used as a weapon), proximity (the batter was very close to the umpire) but he had no evil intent. Thus, there is no criminal act here.

Change the scene. While still at the ball game the batter is upset with the umpire's calls. On the third call of a strike the batter turns and deliberately strikes the umpire with his bat. This is a criminal use of force, because here we have the intent to do harm.

Castle Doctrine Law

More than thirty states now have some form of Castle Doctrine and/or Stand Your Ground law. They vary in wording and the protections offered. As this is being written the states are:

Alabama, Alaska, Arizona, California, Florida, Georgia, Illinois, Indiana, Kansas, Kentucky, Louisiana, Maine, Massachusetts, Michigan, Mississippi, Missouri, Montana, North Carolina, North Dakota, Ohio, Oklahoma, Pennsylvania, Rhode Island, South Carolina, South Dakota, Tennessee, Texas, Utah, West Virginia and Wyoming

Such laws do much to protect a victim of a criminal act from both criminal and civil penalties, so long as the individual acted reasonably and within the bounds of the statute. There are subtle differences among the various states which have such protections, and you would be well advised to know your state's law in regard this matter.

In general, for a person to be covered by one of the Castle Doctrine laws, these facts must be present:

> An intruder must be making (or have made) an attempt to unlawfully and/or forcibly enter an occupied residence, business or vehicle (some states include vehicles under their statutes)
> The intruder must be acting illegally–the Castle Doctrine does not give one the right to attack officers of the law acting in the course of their legal duties
> The occupant(s) of the home must reasonably believe that the intruder intends to inflict serious bodily harm or death upon an occupant of the home, or,

> ➤ the occupant(s) of the home must reasonably believe that the intruder intends to commit some other felony, such as arson or burglary

> ➤ The occupant(s) of the home must not have provoked or instigated an intrusion, or provoked or instigated an intruder to threaten or use deadly force

> ➤ The occupant(s) of the home may be required to attempt to exit the house or otherwise retreat. This is called the "duty to retreat." Most self-defense statutes referred to as examples of the "Castle Doctrine" expressly state that the homeowner has no such duty

In all cases, the occupant(s) of the home must be there *legally*, must not be fugitives from the law, must not be using the Castle Doctrine to aid or abet another person in being a fugitive from the law, and must not use deadly force upon an officer of the law, or an officer of the peace, while they are performing or attempting to perform their legal duties.

A final thought in regard the "when" to use deadly physical force in one's defense. Many years ago I made up this simple analogy; think of danger as arrows (as in bows and arrows). When the arrows are headed your way, use whatever force is necessary to stop those arrows. When the arrows are headed away from you, refrain from using force.

A number of other firearms instructors have picked up and used my "arrows" lesson. It's lots simpler than trying to remember the subtleties of the law!

*

Tactics

The following is a general discussion about some tactical considerations one might take in regard home defense. The subject is far too broad, and requiring of hands on training, to be covered in detail here.

Every situation is going to be different. Some of the many variables to be dealt with are; your nature, and the level of your training and experience, who is in your home at the time of the incident, who the intruder/s are, their mind set and intent, as well as how the house is laid out.

Some basic considerations. Let us assume for the moment that you have access to a firearm (which you know how to use and are familiar with) and;

- ➢ It's 3 AM. You hear a noise in the house that makes you think someone is walking about. (How often do people in your home walk around in a pitch-black house at that hour of the morning?)
- ➢ You gain access to your firearm and flashlight. Do not turn the light on, as you'll be identifying your location to others.
- ➢ Who else should be in the house at that hour?
  Guests
  Family (adults and children)
  Pets
- ➢ Where should the people who belong there be located?
- ➢ If possible, phone the police. For two reasons:
  Get them coming, and,
  put them on notice of the situation you are facing.
- ➢ Round up everyone who should be in the home and bring them to a central location (your bedroom?).
- ➢ Take cover and wait for the arrival of the police, or for the intruder to get to you.
- ➢ Rule of thumb; only search for the intruder if you believe you have no other option.

It is almost always best to remain in your bedroom, set up a good tactical, defensible position for yourself and others, and wait for the police to arrive. If you've called 911, it is generally best to stay on the phone with the dispatcher until officers physically arrive at and secure the scene.

*

Securing firearms in the home:

You don't want to advertise the fact that you have firearms in the home. Now, I realize that different regions of the country will hold different degrees of concern in regard this admonition. None the less, I think it prudent to keep your valuable firearms out of sight, as well as secure them from access by unauthorized individuals. This means, no glass cases showing off one's long arms, no firearms on mantelpieces (OK, maybe a nice muzzle loader would look pretty neat up there), no handguns in glass display boxes.

A good quality safe, bolted to the floor, is the best way to store and secure your firearms. For "house-guns," sidearms for home defense, a small size, good quality biometric safe might be the best way to go.

If you do need some individual firearms to be outside a safe, then consider getting a good quality firearm-lock. Whatever lock you opt for, make sure they are designed for use with keys, not combination locks, which would be all but impossible to open in the event of immediate need (due to the poor lighting, excitement of the moment, etc.).

The absolute worst place to "hide" a firearm is in a bureau draw. Burglars just dump drawers out on the bed or floor looking to see their contents. There's no hiding anything in such places.

*

After the Shooting

Some general guidelines you might consider following after a justified self-defense shooting:

➢ Be polite and courteous to the responding police.
➢ You may be upset. Cry if you are so inclined.
➢ Surrender your firearm if so requested.

232

> ➤ As often as practical state that you wish to speak to or call your attorney.
> ➤ Remain politely "silent." State you've been instructed by your lawyer to wait until you speak to him before going into detail about the incident with anyone else.
> ➤ You won't feel well. You will be in shock. You should see a physician immediately after the incident. Trust me. Ask for immediate medical attention.

***

One final thought; As an armed citizen you are not a law enforcement officer. Your main goal, should you find yourself in the position of having to deal with a dangerous sociopath, an individual who is bent on committing a crime, and who is putting your life at risk, your primary goal is:

To Break Contact!!

You want to get some distance between you and the threat, as quickly as possible. If you can do so without resorting to the use of deadly force, you will be well ahead in such a situation.

References Firearms in the Home and Myths of Self-Defense

[1]The Magliato Case, Mas Ayoob,
http://www.thegunzone.com/ayoob/magliato-ayoob.html

[2]Justices Rule Police Do Not Have a Constitutional Duty to Protect Someone, *NY Times*, June 28, 2005,

http://www.nytimes.com/2005/06/28/politics/28scotus.html?_r=0

[3]No Duty to Protect: Two Exceptions, *The Police Chief, October 2012,*

http://www.policechiefmagazine.org/magazine/index.cfm?fuseaction=
display_arch&article_id=341&issue_id=72004

[4]The Police Have No Obligation to Protect You. Yes, Really., *PJ Media*, December 25, 2011,

http://pjmedia.com/blog/the-police-have-no-obligation-to-protect-you-
yes-really/

Traveling with Firearms

~Via Commercial Aircraft as well as by Private Vehicle~

Executive Summary

Should you attend one of the various firearms training venues offered around the nation you'll certainly want to go there with your personal sidearm. Traveling with firearms in this country is, relative to other nations, a routine matter, so long as you follow some basic, dare I say, common sense rules. This discussion is an overview of how you and your firearms may move about the states with a minimum of hassle and worry.

*

Federal law protects citizen traveling with firearms. The specific section of law relevant to such travel is: **Code of Federal Regulations** Title 18 - Part I - Chapter 44 - § 926a. The entire law may be seen in the Reference Section at the back of this chapter. None the less, there are a number of things you must be aware of when traveling with firearms, whether by aircraft or auto.

*

Travel by Air

Should you opt to travel by air with a firearm I'd urge you show up at the airport with a full two-hour buffer between your arrival time at the airport and the departure time of your flight.

These are the fundamental rules (mostly TSA) which must be complied with:

> ➢ All firearms MUST BE UNLOADED!
> ➢ They must be secured in a hard-sided container (one you can't readily pry open).
> ➢ Firearms MUST BE DECLARED at the airline counter (no curbside luggage pick up!!).
> ➢ The container must be lockable.

➢ You must open the container for the screener, or TSA inspector, as required by them. By federal TSA regulations you must keep possession of the lock's key once the bag/container is cleared by them.

➢ Ammunition must be secured in container(s) designed for the carry of ammunition. Best use factory boxes to avoid confusion.

➢ Loaded magazines are allowed so long as they are secured in a container which completely encloses the ammunition. No exposed primers! (Suggestion: just carry your magazines empty. It will avoid potential –and unnecessary– confusion).

➢ Ammo may be secured in the same hard sided container as the firearm.

➢ Neither black powder nor percussion caps are permitted to be carried either in carry-on, or in checked bags. Such items are not allowed aboard the aircraft, period!

The above is the summary of the TSA regulations. Each airline has its own set of rules. This is no big deal, but it would be most prudent to print out, and keep with you, the regs of the airline you are traveling on. I have some sample airline regulations in the <u>Reference Section</u> at the end of the chapter. When looking for information in regard a specific airline when traveling with firearms I've found all I need do is "Goggle" the name of the airline I'll be flying on along with the word "firearms" (such as; "JetBlue firearms"), and the correct site comes right up.

<u>**Some Things You Ought to Do!**</u>

If you are legal where you start the flight, and legal where you are going, you are all set! Problems arise when you wind up at a destination where you are not lawfully in possession of your firearm/s! I'm thinking of locations such as New York State (especially in NYC), New Jersey and

Illinois. If you inadvertently find yourself in a place you never intended to be in (due to bad weather, mechanical issues aboard the aircraft, whatever) *you are not to take possession of your luggage!* <u>Leave any of your bags containing firearms with the airline!</u>

Furthermore, you have an obligation to know the laws of whatever locale you intend to visit. I've listed the websites for <u>Handgunlaw</u> as well as <u>Pack and Go</u> in the <u>Reference Section</u> at the end of the chapter. These sites contain useful information as to specific locations as well as their laws regarding the possession and carrying of firearms.

You ought to have in your possession, as well as in the hard case in which the firearms are located, copies of both the relevant TSA regulations as well as the airline's regulations. I also suggest that you mark, in yellow marker pen, the most relevant sections of these regulations. This is so that should you need to show the regulations to either an airline employee, or a TSA representative, their eyes will quickly fall to the most important sections of the relevant laws and regulations.

You don't want to embarrass them! My tack is, upon seeing some confusion on the part of an airline employee, to calmly say, "These regs sure are confusing. That's why I keep copies of them with me," and then gently hand the copies over to the person in question. Works wonders.

<u>Dealing With Airline Personnel</u>

I've never had a truly bad experience during air travel when declaring I have an unloaded handgun. And, no, I generally do not now identify myself as a retired police officer (nor did I routinely ID myself as an active law officer when I was still on active duty) when checking my baggage in. But, there's always tomorrow.

My suggestion, when you first encounter the airline representative at the counter is;

Smile (really), and state, in a calm, soft voice, "Hi. I'd like to declare an **unloaded** handgun." I have found that this technique of emphasizing the word **unloaded**, during the initial interaction with the counter person, puts people at ease.

Here is what is most likely to happen next;

> ➤ You will be handed a small piece of paper (a form) to sign. This paper will travel with your firearm in your baggage.
> ➤ The airline employee will (should) ask to see that the firearm is unloaded. Sometimes, they simply ask.
> ➤ Once they are confident that the guns are unloaded, they will have you re-secure the luggage and, either move the luggage over to the TSA, or, have a TSA person inspect the firearms in a private room (they've done that to me when at Boston's Logan airport).
> ➤ Once the luggage is finally taken from you, you should next see it (and your firearms) at your destination airport.

When you land, the custom now is to have you pick up your luggage, specifically the bag containing the firearm, from that airline's baggage claim office. That location should be near the baggage carousel.

Might I offer one bit of advice. Consider purchasing a "traveling" handgun if you wish to routinely carry a concealed firearm during your trips. I bought a Ruger LCR for this purpose. I think a Charter Arms revolver would also do nicely, perhaps even a Taurus or Rossi. There is nothing wrong with these handguns. In fact, both the Ruger LCR, and the Charter Arms handgun I own I've found to be good, honest and reliable pieces of machinery. It's simply that, to me, they are tools. If I lose my Ruger LCR, I'll just go buy another.

The Gun Case

Here's what I use;

> ➢ I have a Pelican hard sided case, which is;
> ➢ Connected to the luggage via a plastic-coated metal cable.
> ➢ The cable is attached to the frame of the luggage.

This may be a bit of overkill, but it makes me happy. The Pelican case is very robust. By securing it to the cable, which is attached to the luggage, I have enhanced the secure transport of my firearm. Is it foolproof? Nothing is. But, unless the bad guy has a bolt cutter in his back pocket, he's going to have a real problem making away with my gun case.

By regulation, all you need is a securable, lockable, hard sided container to hold the firearm. Many modern handguns now come sold in hard plastic cases with a hole (or holes) in the handle designed for the use of a hasp lock. These are perfectly OK to use when traveling with a firearm, according to the TSA. Be warned; If your case has two holes for locks, some airline employees insist both locks must be in place.

Keep in mind, whatever case you opt to use, if you can easily pry the sides open, you stand a good chance of not being permitted to board the aircraft with the firearm in your luggage! Buy a good case.

*

Demonstrating that the Handgun is Unloaded

This has the potential to cause confusion. The person asking to see that the firearm is unloaded very likely has no idea on how to handle a firearm. Indeed, most of the time they won't touch your gun. The trick is to demonstrate to them that the handgun is unloaded in an unobtrusive a manner as possible.

If you're carrying a semi-automatic pistol, you might consider having the gun broken down into two parts. There is little room left to debate as to whether or not a firearm is loaded when seeing a disassembled handgun. If you opt for a revolver (as I frequently do), I suggest a good quality trigger lock be attached to the handgun, while it's in the gun case!

If You Run Into a Jerk

Don't become upset, angry, loud or condescending (*"Do you know who I am?"*). Remain calm, act in a professional and controlled fashion. Know the law and regulations. Have copies of both the TSA and airline's regulations readily available to share with the person you are dealing with. If all else fails, respectfully request to speak to a supervisor.

What Should You Know?

At minimum, you should be aware that:

➢ Flying with an unloaded firearm is not difficult.
➢ All you really need is a securable hard sided container to hold the firearm.
➢ Ammunition should best be carried in its factory box.
➢ Give yourself plenty of time when arriving at the airport. You'll be much less tense about the whole transaction, and, you'll also have a great excuse to eat the grossly overpriced fast food offerings at the airport.

*

Traveling by Privately Owned Vehicle

Each state has a different set of laws which control how one may be in lawful possession of a firearm, especially a handgun, during travel through that locale. As a general rule, so long as you are in continuous and uninterrupted travel through the difficult states (mostly in the northeastern part of the nation) all will be well.

None the less, in my opinion the most prudent way to travel through "hostile" territory is:

> If taking a semiautomatic pistol, break it down into at least two parts.
> If a revolver, have a trigger lock attached to the handgun.
> Secure your revolver in a locked hard sided container.
> If a semi-auto pistol, lock the two parts of the handgun in two separate containers.
> Secure your ammunition in a separate, locked, container.
> Have all locks keyed the same (ACE Hardware sells sets of hasp-type locks all keyed the same. I'm sure other hardware stores offer this option as well.)
> Have a copy of the federal laws pertaining to traveling with a firearm readily available.
> Consider having the "difficult" State's regulations printed out as well.
> Lock all firearms and ammunition in the trunk of your vehicle.

Permit me to be blunt; when was the last time a police officer conducted a search of your private vehicle? Most probably the answer is, never. The most likely reason for the question as to whether or not you are in lawful possession of firearms would be in the event you are in a motor vehicle accident, become ill or disabled, and/or your vehicle becomes impounded. Those are the most probable situations which may lead to some legal issue arising in regard your transporting firearms.

Do keep in mind that some states have very strict laws in regard magazine capacity. New York limits you to ten round magazines (with only seven rounds permitted to be carried in it!), New Jersey fifteen round magazines. I have no great answer to this conundrum. When on the road I secure my magazines, empty and locked away from any ammunition, in my car's locked trunk.

If you insist on having high-capacity magazines at your destination, and are concerned in regard this issue, you might consider mailing them from where you're starting the trip to where you'll be going to (or even buy a couple while you're there). While traveling to and from simply limit yourself to ten round capacity magazines. Just a thought.

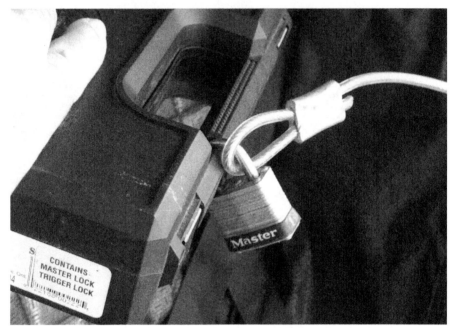

Cable Attached to Hasp Lock

Do keep in mind that every encounter with a law enforcement officer will be unique. Attitudes toward civilian ownership of firearms will vary with individual officers. Furthermore, not every officer is fully aware of the law in regard the lawful transport of firearms. Most encounters would likely result in no unpleasant consequences. Most often, your attitude will, to a greater or lesser degree, be the controlling factor as to the end result of the interaction. On the other hand, life is not necessarily fair, just or logical.

Refer to the sites in the Reference Section for Handgun Law and Pack and Go for information as it relates to the law in specific locations in the United States.

*

In the photo on the previous page you can see that I've attached the hasp lock and cable to a hard side factory S&W handgun box, the version with a hole in the handle designed to comply with TSA regulations for air travel. The cable was already secured through the frame of the luggage. Obviously, large handgun cases would be secured the same way.

~

Travel with Firearms Reference Section

Code of Federal Regulations *Title 18 - Part I - Chapter 44 - § 926a*

Release date: 2005-08-03

Notwithstanding any other provision of any law or any rule or regulation of a State or any political subdivision thereof, any person who is not otherwise prohibited by this chapter from transporting, shipping, or receiving a firearm shall be entitled to transport a firearm for any lawful purpose from any place where he may lawfully possess and carry such firearm to any other place where he may lawfully possess and carry such firearm if, during such transportation the firearm is unloaded, and neither the firearm nor any ammunition being transported is readily accessible or is directly accessible from the passenger compartment of such transporting vehicle: Provided, that in the case of a vehicle without a compartment separate from the driver's compartment the firearm or ammunition shall be contained in a locked container other than the glove compartment or console.

*

Handgun Law website:

> http://handgunlaw.us/

*

Pack and Go website:

http://apps.carryconcealed.net/packngo/

*

Glocktalk "Sticky" on traveling by air with a firearm. Good information here as well:

http://glocktalk.com/forums/showthread.php?t=1202384

*

TSA Regulations

Firearms and Ammunition

Firearms, ammunition and firearm parts may only be transported in checked baggage. Firearms, ammunition and firearm parts are prohibited from carry-on baggage.

There are certain limited exceptions for law enforcement officers (LEOs) who are authorized to fly armed by meeting the requirements of 49 CFR § 1544.219.

Following is a summary of key regulatory requirements to transport firearms, firearm parts or ammunition in checked baggage:

- All firearms **must be declared to the air carrier** during the ticket counter check-in process.
- The firearm must be **unloaded**.
- The firearm must be carried in a **hard-sided container**.
- The container must be **locked**.
- The passenger must provide the key or combination to the screener if it is necessary to open the container, and then remain present during screening to **take back possession of the key after the container is cleared.**
- Any ammunition transported must be securely packed in fiber (such as cardboard), wood or metal **boxes or other packaging specifically designed to carry small amounts of ammunition.**
- **Firearm magazines/clips** do not satisfy the packaging requirement unless they provide a **complete and secure enclosure of the ammunition** (e.g., by securely covering the exposed portions of the magazine or by securely placing the magazine in a pouch, holder, holster or lanyard).
- The **ammunition may** also be located in the **same hard-sided case as the firearm**, as long as it is properly packed as described above.
- **Black powder and percussion caps** used with black-powder type firearms are **not permitted** in carry-on or checked baggage.

The regulations are strictly enforced. Violations can result in criminal prosecution and the imposition of civil penalties of up to $10,000 per violation.

Air carriers may have their own additional requirements in regard the carriage of firearms as well as the amount of ammunition an individual may place in checked baggage. Therefore, travelers should also **contact the air carrier regarding its firearm and ammunition carriage policies.**

If you are traveling with a gun or ammunition, please read our information on traveling with these items for more information. Traveling with Firearms and Ammunition

This is the link:

http://www.tsa.gov/travelers/airtravel/assistant/editorial_1666.shtm

*

Delta Regulations

Pistols

You can bring pistols and accessories as checked baggage as long as they are included in one pistol case and contain:

- Pistol telescopes
- Noise suppressers
- A small pistol tool case
- No more than 11 lbs. (5 kg) of ammunition

Please read important information regarding packaging and presenting/declaring firearms at check-in.

Rifles and Shotguns

Delta will accept firearms and shooting equipment packaged as follows:

- One-gun case containing rifles or shotguns, plus shooting materials, and tools

- One-gun case containing handguns, one scope, and tools
- One bow and quiver of arrows and maintenance kit enclosed in a case or container of sufficient strength to protect the bow and quiver from accidental damage

An excess baggage fee will apply if checking more than one-gun case. Ammunition is limited to 11 lbs. (5 kg).

*

Southwest Airlines

Guns and Ammunition

Guns

- Customers are responsible for knowing and following the firearms laws of the state(s) that they will be traveling **to, from, and through.**
- Our Customers must declare the gun to the Customer Service Agent at the ticket counter (no firearms will be accepted curbside) and ensure that the firearm(s) chambers are free of ammunition and the magazine clip has been removed (when applicable). Paintball guns and BB guns are considered the same as all other firearms.
- Paintball guns are allowed in checked baggage and are not subject to the container requirements of firearms. Customers must declare the paintball gun to the Customer Service Agent at the ticket counter. Compressed gas cylinders are allowed in checked baggage or as a carryon only if the regulator valve is completely disconnected from the cylinder and the cylinder is no longer sealed (i.e., the cylinder has an open end). TSA Security Screeners must visibly ensure that the cylinder is completely empty and that there are no prohibited items inside.
- Firearms must be encased in a hard-sided, **locked** container that is of sufficient strength to withstand normal handling, as follows:

1. A firearm in a hard-sided, locked container may be placed inside a soft-sided, unlocked suitcase.
2. A firearm placed inside a hard-sided, locked suitcase does not have to be encased in a container manufactured for the transportation of firearms.
3. The locked container or suitcase must completely secure the firearm from access. Cases or suitcases that can be pulled open with minimal effort do not meet the locked criterion.
4. Only the Customer checking the luggage should retain the key or combination to the lock. **No exceptions will be made.**

- Firearms may be checked and will count toward the two-piece free baggage allowance for each fare-paying passenger. We allow multiple firearms to be transported inside one hard-sided case.
- Southwest Airlines assumes no liability for the misalignment of sights on firearms, including those equipped with telescopic sights.
- Firearms are never allowed in carryon luggage.

Ammunition

- Small arms ammunition for personal use (provided it is properly packed) is permissible in checked baggage only.
- The ammunition may be placed in the same container as the firearm and must be securely packed in cardboard (fiber), wood, or metal boxes, or other packaging specifically designed to carry small amounts of ammunition.
- When checking ammunition, Customers are limited to 11 pounds gross weight (ammunition plus container) per person.
- Magazines or clips containing ammunition must be securely packaged (placed in another small box or in a secure cutout in

the carrying case, in order to protect the primer of the ammunition).

- Make sure guns are unloaded and definitely never transport a gun in your carryon baggage!
- Gunpowder (black powder) and primers or percussion caps are not allowed in checked or carryon baggage.
- Loose ammunition or loose loaded magazines and/or clips are not allowed.
- Paintballs must be packaged in a leak-proof container and will be conditionally accepted.

*

Printed in Great Britain
by Amazon

25849422R00145